The Use of Force in Modern Policing

By Richard Rosenthal

Chief Wellfleet MA Police Department, retired

Lieutenant, New York City Police Department, retired

Richard Rosenthal

Other books by the author:

The Murder of Old Comrades

Sky Cops

K-9 Cops

*Rookie Cop, Deep Undercover in the JDL
(Jewish Defense League)*

Practical Handgun Training

Self-Publishing ~ Simplified!

The Third Nation

Available from: **_Amazon_**

Contact the author at:

RichWellfleet@Comcast.net

ISBN: #13: 978-1541344716

Contents

Richard Rosenthal

Introduction to The Use of Force in Modern Policing

"There is more law in the end of a policeman's nightstick then in a decision of the Supreme Court."

Captain Alexander S. ("Clubber") Williams, Late 19th Century
New York City Police Department

This book could well be summarized in a sentence:

When enforcing the law police officers may use that degree of force which is reasonable, necessary, and appropriate in order to bring about compliance with the law, as well as use that amount of force required to be employed in order to take a person into custody.

It is remarkable that such a simple concept as the lawful use of force by law enforcement officers can be the basis for such national consternation.

It was not that long ago that the use of force by police officers went virtually unchallenged, as might be surmised by the quote seen above from "Clubber" Williams a century ago. Today policing has never been more difficult, under more intense scrutiny, or engendered such a degree of controversy within the United States. Police, mostly street level uniformed forces, are under more public oversight than has ever taken place in prior history. It seems to matter little to their critics whether officers are "right" or "wrong" in their interactions with the public, most especially when the use of force is involved and most assuredly when Deadly Physical Force is employed. Public criticism is often vocal, one sided and in many cases perpetrating fictions as to what had really taken place during the actual situations which occurred when the officers had to use force to deal with the circumstances at hand. In truth, officers are finding less and less support from the very people they are sworn to protect. This conundrum not only puts the officers at greater risk of injury but detracts from their ability to protect the greater public.

4

There is no such thing as the "nice-looking" use of force. In our society we are inundated with movies and television programs depicting police/citizen interactions. But life is not a set-piece television show or carefully scripted and rehearsed movie scene. In the majority of these yarns several factors hold sway; we as the audience know in advance who the "bad" guys as well as the "evil" guys are. Those roles are clearly set out for us. We know as well who the good guys are, those noble, brave, physically imposing, virtually indestructible but sometimes emotionally flawed heroes who will, in the end, prevail against the malefactors of the world and right all evils.

How we are aware of these things is quite simple; everyone involved in the story follows a script. The good guys know who they are, the bad guys are mindful of their roles and the victims are also tuned in to their relationship with everyone involved. Regrettably, and certainly during my forty years as an active law enforcement officer, while on duty I never came upon any scene in which I already knew who the "actors" were or what "parts" they played in the dramas unfolding before me. And there lies the rub, recognized by the supreme court's ruling on the police use of force, *Graham v. Connor*; whatever force is used by a lawman must be viewed through the eyes of a reasonable police officer based on the objective reality of the immediate situation faced by them at the moment of the interaction.

When interviewing Sergeant Brian Kowalski of the Tucson Police Department, he pointed out that the current police practice, of hiring individuals from a segment of society that has little experience in the use of physical force against others (even a modest history of physical confrontations would be a disqualifier for most departments), has some serious downsides. He pointed out that his rookie officers rarely have had to punch someone since grade school, yet must deal with members of society where physical violence is a

5

way of life. He suggested these new recruits are in "for a sharp learning curve."

Our current police training emphasizes to new officers the perils of their abusing the use of force, with the real risks of loss of their police position or even incarceration. He finds this to be a symptom of an out of balance society, that we do this to the people we give the power of arrest to, give them badges and gives them guns as well.

Examples of the horrendous decisions officers must make, and the consequences of their aftermath, play out all too frequently. Only a short time since writing these words a police officer, responding to a report of an armed robbery, drove up to the scene and observed three young men fitting the description of the perpetrators. Two of the young men fled. One, for reasons I do not know, stood his ground and, again for reasons I cannot fathom, responded to the officer's commands by reaching into his belt and withdrawing a simulated handgun, impossible to distinguish from an actual firearm but none the less referred to by those criticizing the officers' actions as a "BB" gun. The officer opened fire, killing a twelve-year-old child.

Without having all the complex facts of that situation before me I cannot offer up any reasoned commentary on the officers' actions. I simply recall, that when working in narcotics enforcement in the Bronx, I once grabbed a young man on the street, someone who had just sold heroin to an undercover police officer. My prisoner was fourteen and was armed with a fully loaded pistol.

Violent confrontations between combatants is a primal exercise, where both parties are, to a greater or lesser degree, fighting for their lives. Hand to hand combat is never pretty. There are damn few rules, the main one being, "Survive the encounter."

When the amount of force used by police rises to the level of Deadly Physical Force then the visual and visceral horrors of the scene are magnified. People, when shot, do not swoon gently into that good night, uttering some profound and moving sentiment such as, "Tell mom I loved her." After the shooting, "Monday Morning Quarterbacks," not subject to the dangers of the moment, or the rush of adrenaline which comes when engaged in such an exercise, and most often possessing knowledge now which none of the officers involved in the incident had when facing the situation at the time of the event, will expound on what the police at the scene should have done, often parsing the actions performed by the officers down to fractions of seconds, as if a person under such trying circumstances could actually make reasoned judgements with such rapidity.

In short, police officers are frequently required to make split-second decisions on matters of life and death involving unique situations they had never contemplated nor anticipated becoming embroiled in. The question society must deal with is, how much latitude are we to allow our law officers in their decision making? How can we guide them in the processing of an infinite number of variables, most often coming upon the officers with little or no warning. With many of these situations where the outcome will impact their lives, their careers, indeed, their very freedom, should they be judged to have erred.

In this book I've struggled to discuss this terribly complex matter in a reasoned, somewhat dispassionate way as well as from the perspective of my own empirical experiences, which I garnered during my over forty year police career. This is my way of saying that I have attempted to make this work a readable one, while at the same time recognizing the legal, moral, ethical and tactical complexities of the use of force issue. While there may be a plethora of data available which discuss various aspects of the police use of force (the *Federal Bureau of Investigations Officers Killed* annual report as well as the New York City Police Department's annual *Firearms Discharge Report*, formerly referred to as SOP-9, are but two such useful sources regarding this subject) my reviewing such material quickly led me to the conclusion that my readers eyes would soon glaze over if I inserted too much cold statistical data into this work. None the less, some numbers and the reference to statistical data are necessary for the reader to be cognizant of, in order for them to understand the issues being discussed. I've done my best to keep such dry material out of this book to the extent reasonable.

The Ubiquitous Video Camera

I would venture to say that few changes in our technological lives have impacted law enforcement (and, arguably, our military as well) to the degree as have the now ubiquitous video camera (in all its iterations; cell phones, smart phones, stand-alone cameras, surveillance cameras, etc.). And, as with all new changes in society, along with the technology come some adjustments in the "way things are done."

There was a time when a contested confrontation between a law enforcement officer and a citizen was decided based on the word of the officer, which carried far more weight than that of the other party involved in the brouhaha. Now we are all seeing that, often, there are at least three sides to the story; the citizen's, the officer's, and the video recording of the event. Frequently the three tales differ markedly. I suspect there are a number of reasons for the discrepancies. When a person, either an individual doing something "bad" or an officer when enforcing the law, is directly involved in a physical confrontation there is a natural tendency to develop what is commonly referred to as "tunnel vision." I am aware of numerous police shootings where, when the officers involved were later questioned, they reported firing far fewer rounds than were in fact expended. They weren't lying, the individuals involved simply were incapable of incorporating this information into their conscious minds during the period of intense physical and psychological stimulation and saturation they had been embroiled in. In short, they were human beings and thus limited in their ability to take note of what was going on around them during a life and death struggle.

Videos may be quite accurate or, counterintuitively, very misleading, dependent on the camera's angle of view and when the recording was started. Multiple recordings of an event are invariably more edifying when investigators are parsing out the actual facts of an incident.

I urge the reader to be objective in regard policing and video cameras. How would your job performance be impacted if half a dozen people stood off to the side as you were performing your work and recorded your actions on their "smartphones?" Would you find that to be a bit off-putting perhaps? I am not so naïve as to believe the recording of public events will somehow be lessened in the future, but must wonder as to how this new ubiquity of such recordings will impact the larger society.

Chapter 1~
How Did We Get to Where We Are?

A Short History of Policing in the United States

"We sleep soundly in our beds while rough men stand ready in the night to do violence upon those who would cause us harm."

Edmund Burke

Our nation has been in existence for roughly two and a half centuries. The basic understanding of how we, as a people, are "policed" has dramatically evolved over time. I suggest it is important to our understanding of how this country's law officers now comport themselves among the citizenry, as well as how those tasked with enforcing our laws are allowed and permitted to use force, be examined in light of our history in this regard.

Permit me to preface this chapter by explaining that some of the material contained here comes from a dissertation (an Abstract) authored by Roger Roots, printed in the Seton Hall Constitutional L.J.[1]

This discussion is primarily limited to our nation's municipal, county and state law enforcement agencies. Federal agencies have evolved, to a great extent, on another track entirely.

Data from *"U.S. State and Local Law Enforcement Agencies Census 2008"* by Bureau of Justice Statistics show that in this nation there were, when that report came out: [2]

- ➤ 12,501 local police departments
- ➤ 3,063 sheriffs' offices
- ➤ 50 primary state law enforcement agencies
- ➤ 1,733 special jurisdiction agencies
- ➤ 683 other agencies, primarily county constable offices in Texas.

This census reported that there were 251 sworn law officers (not counting those assigned to federal agencies – a not insignificant number) per 100,000 citizens. This translates to the number of non-federal enforcement personnel in our country being more than approximately 900,000 people (admittedly a number of dubious accuracy).[3]

When our nation began there were no organized municipal law enforcement agencies.[4] As foreign as the idea may be to us now, the role of law enforcement during the early period of our nation's history was quite restricted, the few state authorized enforcement officers which then existed were basically limited to "executive" functions of the law; warrants, court orders, writs and such.[5]

Remarkably, the enforcement and investigation of criminal law was under the purview of the citizenry. Beginning in the 1630s Boston

Night Watchmen During the Colonial Period

became the first settlement (it certainly wasn't a "city" back then) employing a Night Watchman.[6] New York followed in 1658 and Philadelphia in 1700.[7] The function of these men (they were all male

11

forces) was likely more for public safety purposes, such as keeping watch for fires, Indian raids, as well as for strangers wandering into the community.[8]

Around the time our Constitution was ratified sheriffs were appointed and constables were either elected or drafted from their community to serve without pay.[9] The enforcement of laws, such as it was, fell to the citizenry of the period. It is necessary to look to England and Sir Robert Peel for the creation of the first "modern day" institution of organized policing. Sir Robert, during the 1820s when serving as Home Secretary, created London's Metropolitan police force. While otherwise "unarmed," the police personnel of the period did carry a wooden truncheon.[10]

In 1838, Boston formed the first municipal police department in the United States, followed by New York City in 1845. By the latter part of the 19th Century all major cities in this country had municipal police forces. It was during this period that a different philosophy evolved, one which diverged from the English system of policing. For complex reasons this nation's police force, acting under color of law, enforced the will (laws) as desired by those in political power. Prior to this, policing, when done at all, was reactive in nature. When there was a violation of law an action was taken. During the 19th century police began to enforce laws and protect citizens against "bad" people; drunkards, "dope fiends," the homeless or anyone designated as a "dangerous class" of person. Ours was a different model than the English system. The English feared intrusive law enforcement, police surveillance and furtive observation. Indeed, Peel went out of his way, when forming his London police unit, to dress "his" officers in as unintimidating an appearance as possible, as far from a uniform as was practical yet in a manner to distinguish this group of citizens from those around them.

***The Members of the Two 19th Century NYPDs Fighting for
Control~ Municipals versus Metropolitans***

The New York City Police Department is a case in point; the police
were appointed by local political leaders and were there to do the
bidding of those same people.

Walker (1996) tells us:

"Police (in New York City) systematically took payoffs to allow
illegal drinking, gambling and prostitution. Police organized
professional criminals, like thieves and pickpockets, trading
immunity for bribes or information. They actively participated in
vote-buying and ballot-box-stuffing. Loyal political operatives
became police officers. They had no discernable qualifications for
policing and little if any training in policing. Promotions within the
police departments were sold, not earned. Police drank while on
patrol, they protected their patron's vice operations, and they were
quick to use peremptory force."

Furthermore, the police were used to quell labor disputes during this period. According to Dr. Gary Potter, there were over 5,000 strikes in the city during the latter part of the 19th century. Police were authorized to use force against these strikers.

Dr. Potter suggests that there were three major issues which 19th century police departments faced:

> ➢ Should police be uniformed?
> ➢ Should they carry firearms? And, most germane to this discussion,
> ➢ How much force ought police be permitted to use to carry out their duties?

Prior to officers officially being armed by their departments, officers took it upon themselves to carry firearms. None the less, there was a debate then, as now, on just how much force our police should be authorized to use in the lawful performance of their duty. Much of the force which was used was aimed at those with the least amount of political and social power; immigrants, freed slaves, inebriants. The ruling class prevailed, because, according to Bordua and Reiss (1967):

The presence of a paramilitary force, occupying the streets, was regarded as essential because such "organizations intervened between the propertied elites and property less masses who were regarded as politically dangerous as a class."

Dr. Potter writes this unsettling account of how and why some of our state police agencies came into being:

State police agencies emerged for many of the same reasons. The Pennsylvania State Police were modeled after the Philippine Constabulary, the occupation force placed in the Philippine Islands following the Spanish-American War. This all-white, all-"native" paramilitary force was created specifically to break strikes in the coal fields of Pennsylvania and to control local towns composed predominantly of Catholic, Irish, German and Eastern European immigrants. They were housed in barracks outside the towns so that they would not mingle with or develop friendships with local residents. In addition to strike-breaking they frequently engaged in anti-immigrant and anti-Catholic violence, such as attacking community social events on horseback, under the pretense of enforcing public order laws. Similarly, the Texas Rangers were originally created as a quasi-official group of vigilantes and guerillas used to suppress Mexican communities and to drive the Comanche off their lands.

Then, soon after, came the Prohibition laws (1919~1933). The police were faced with enforcing laws ignored by a clear majority of United States citizens. This not only caused tremendous social conflict between citizenry and the enforcers of these unwanted laws, but created a fertile ground for massive police corruption, not to mention the creation of powerful (politically as well as financially) organized crime entities. In some ways the American police officer (along with our political establishment) became extensions of the well-structured crime syndicates.

The juxtaposition of how our nation comported itself during the Prohibition era demonstrates an eerily similar pattern as to how we as a nation are currently dealing with our War on Drugs. We will come back to discuss the War on Drugs later in the book.

When police officers are tasked with enforcing criminal statutes against popular, socially accepted acts; prostitution, gambling, drinking, consuming various recreational chemical substances– the soil is fertile for corruption. Few large city police agencies involved in such enforcement activities escape unscathed. Just to list some of the more well-known scandals:

- ➢ Lenox Committee, formed in 1894 to investigate police corruption related to gambling and prostitution and to investigate charges of police extortion. The Lenox

Committee determined that promotion within the New York City Police Department required a bribe of $1,600 to be promoted to sergeant and up to $15,000 to be promoted to Captain. That amount of money was of far greater worth than our inflation ravaged dollars of today. (in 2015 dollars $1,600 then = $43,700 current dollars)

➢ The formation of a prostitution syndicate by Los Angeles Mayor Arthur Harper, Police Chief Edward Kerns, and a local organized crime figure, combined with subsequent instructions to the police to harass this syndicate's competitors in the prostitution industry.

➢ The assassination of organized crime figure Arnold Rothstein by police lieutenant Charles Becker, head of the NYPD's vice squad.

➢ A dispute between the Mayor and District Attorney of Philadelphia, each of whom controlled rival gambling syndicates and each of whom used loyal factions of police to harass the other group (Fogelson 1977: Potter and Jenkins, 1985).

➢ The Curren Committee (1913), which investigated police collusion with gambling and prostitution.

➢ The Seabury Committee (1932), which investigated Prohibition-related corruption.

➢ The 1949 Brooklyn grand jury which investigated gambling payoffs.

➢ The 1972 Knapp Commission which investigated corruption related to gambling and drugs.

➢ The 1993 Mollen Commission which exposed massive drug corruption, organized theft by police officers, excessive use of force, and use of drugs by the police (Kappeler, Sluder and Alpert 1998).

As this book is being prepared (2016/2017) a number of high ranking New York City Police Officers have been charged with assorted acts of malfeasance (in one instance involving the services of a prostitute during a flight by private jet provided by their benefactor) stemming from, among other violations of the public trust, the selling of permits to carry concealed handguns in the city, the acquisition of which is otherwise, for all practical purposes, a lawful impossibility for the average citizen to obtain.

In the period from 1969 to 1972 "someone" signed out of the New York City Police Department's Property Clerk's office four hundred pounds of heroin and cocaine, replacing the multimillion dollar drug stash ($70 million dollars back when the theft took place. To be accurate, narcotics from other cases were also pilfered during the same period.) with flour. No one was ever charged with a crime in this matter.[11, 12, 13]

Much of the responsibility for these lapses among our enforcement officers falls at the feet of our political leaders, who have promulgated laws that are either viewed with disdain by the majority of citizens, go counter to the public's will, or are put in place to enforce breeches in morality that have little or nothing to do with protecting the public. Prohibitions against prostitution comes to mind. Instead of recognizing that human beings will forever engage in sexual activity, whether paid for or of a consensual nature, for many years our political leaders have put laws on the books making what virtually the entire population, one way or another, does on a regular basis, a violation of law. They then assign their police to enforce these absurd laws, which are, in any case, unenforceable, and then are shocked, shocked, to discover informal pecuniary relationships are formed between the purveyors of paid sexual favors and the enforcement arm of the government.

Indeed, when as a young detective in the New York City Police Department I recall conversations with senior detectives who would explain to me how the police department used to keep both houses of prostitution and gamblers within strict limits and under police oversight, by developing an unsanctioned relationship with the vendors of these "vices" and thus having virtual complete management control over when, where and who was conducting these trades. Not a perfect system to be sure, but it served the purpose during that earlier time.

Roger Roots tells us that there is no provision within our nation's Constitution for the enforcement of criminal law. Indeed, according to this author, it was fundamentally the duty of each citizen to act as the enforcers of law. It would appear the founding fathers were more fearful of a powerful government than rampant criminality. I am dubious that such a free-for-all system would now function smoothly in our complex modern society, I'm simply sharing the history of how our police have evolved over time and wish to communicate this information to my readers.

Root states the following in his dissertation:

"(1) victims of serious crimes approached a community grand jury, (2) the grand jury investigated the matter and issued an indictment only if it concluded that a crime should be charged, and (3) the victim himself or his representative (generally an attorney but sometimes a state attorney general) prosecuted the defendant before a petit jury of twelve men. Criminal actions were only a step away from civil actions — the only material difference being that criminal claims ostensibly involved an interest of the public at large as well as the victim."

While the history of our earliest philosophies in regard the enforcement of our laws is interesting I think it important to move on to view our nation's first significant size police agencies.

Two hundred years ago the very term "police" had a different meaning during this earlier time, indicating the watching or monitoring of some activity or action.[14]

During the historical period of Alexis de Tocqueville, a Frenchman writing about his visit to the United States during the early part of the 19th century (1831). He observed that in this nation violations of crime was handled by citizens and, furthermore, he noted an absence of obvious government authority on the streets of this new nation.[15]

During the mid-part of the 19th century, while our nation might well have been primarily an agrarian society, its cities were rapidly growing. It is axiomatic to any experienced police officer, and most certainly has been my empirical observation, that once you put large numbers of disparate people in close proximity, societal behavior deteriorates and acts we define as "criminal" increase. The need for structured, organized protectors of society was born. Thus came the newest iteration of the Roman Centurion to our nation.

Police then, as they very much do now, serve as "generalists" for the purposes of seeing to the welfare of the public. Much more of policing involves dealing with the minutiae of life than do other public entities, which either cannot or will not assist people in their dealing with their infinite number of life problems. I have personally found this to be true while serving at various times in both in the New York City Police Department, our nation's largest police agency, and when as chief of the small Cape Cod town of Wellfleet's Police Department. Some examples follow:

In Wellfleet, a number of winters ago, the town was engulfed in, by Cape Cod standards, a serious snow storm. Sitting in my office I received a phone call from a woman who, at that moment, was at her mother's home in the nearby town of Eastham. The power had been out for some time, the house she was in was therefore unlivable due to the cold. A friend of hers in Wellfleet offered to let the woman and her dog stay in her friend's, but she had to get there first. I called the Eastham Police Department, who sent a cruiser to the woman, managed to get her, her dog and her "stuff" out of the home she was in, over snowbanks and into the Eastham police cruiser. She was then driven to the border of Wellfleet and Eastham, to be transferred to a Wellfleet cruiser.

My cruiser (a four-wheel drive SUV), operated by two of my officers, moved her and her things into the police vehicle and drove off to her friend's residence in Wellfleet. My officers (both women), once there, saw that no path existed in the deep snow which would permit access to the front door of the home from the street! The two officers took out shovels from the rear of the cruiser and dug a path for the woman, her dog and the myriad of things she had brought along with her. There was no other government agency that could have accomplished this task as quickly, as logically and with the lack of fuss, as the police department.

On another occasion a dog was hit by a car on Route 6 (our one and only major north/south road) in Wellfleet. The dog wore a decorative bandana around its neck but bore no other identification. I was at the scene and saw that the animal was in desperate condition. I called my wife to the incident, put the dog in our private car and, with lights and siren blaring from my cruiser, led my wife to the vet some ten or so miles away in Eastham. We carried the dog inside and the animal survived, the vet telling us the dog would have certainly died had it not been brought to them as quickly as it had. Once more, there was no other government entity that could have performed this task. Oh, and we eventually located the dog's owner, who was most appreciative of our actions.

The New York City Police Department routinely, during my years there, dealt with lost and confused souls, animal control issues, broken pipes (gas and water), inebriated persons, traffic issues and on and on with an unending list of often impossible to anticipate problems that citizens found themselves confronted with and for which they had virtually no recourse.

The early model of the New York City Police Department was somewhat unique. Understand, there were two separate police departments in the city for a period during the mid-19th century, the Municipal Police and the Metropolitan Police. This was due to the political powers of the day each wishing to exert control over their illicit fiefdoms and thus requiring the aid of "their" respective police departments of the era. The two departments eventually merged. These forces were modeled heavily after the English system designed by Sir Robert Peel. Indeed, there were debates in regard what uniforms, if any, the members of an organized police force in New York City ought to wear. Many officers objected to the very thought of a formalized uniform, saying this, "conflicted with their notions of independence and self-respect," as well as effectively creating the establishment of a standing Army. The fear of the police becoming a *de-facto* military presence may be seen running through the philosophies and concerns of our founding fathers, the English Parliament when eventually authorizing their first uniformed police force in that country, and our nation's citizens and police officers alike, when debating this topic.

Up to this point in the discussion I have been focusing on the larger law enforcement agencies which came into existence in the United States during the 19th century. The fact is, styles of policing, the amount and type of force that was lawful and acceptable for officers to use against citizens, varied, and varies, dramatically, depending on which part of the nation is being examined, even down to the cultural differences within subsets of these diverse dispersed jurisdictions. A true and comprehensive overview of how these multitudinous police agencies differ in the manner in which they enforce the law as well as their accepted and routine use of force is well beyond the scope of this work.

None the less, I think it necessary to examine, even if in a cursory manner, as to how the "taming of the West" entered into our societal subconscious and, knowingly or by chance, led to citizens' expectations as to how law enforcement should handle "bad hombres."

21

Richard Rosenthal

The myth of the Western hero, the good guy, wearing a white hat, only shooting to wound, never shooting a bad guy in the back, never uttering an inappropriate expletive and acting only in the most chivalrous and gentlemanly fashion when among the weaker sex, is the great American myth. For me, that reality had to be factual as, while growing up during the 1950s and 1960s, watching then current as well as older movies and the then new television programs about the "old West," such was the information presented to me. This is not a pejorative viewpoint on my part as all societies create the realities they wish themselves to believe in.

The truth of the matter is far grittier. The people of our frontier lived the lives they needed to in order to survive in the tough environment which existed during that time and place. The named heroes –and

Hollywood tells it one way... the truth is a mite more complicated.

Our "Myth" of the Western Hero Lawman

Lawmen of the 19th Century
Note the Man in Chains on the Left~Their Prize

lawmen– of the period often led far more sordid lives then their biographers and tellers of tales would like us to believe. Wyatt Earp served as a bouncer in brothels, was a saloon-keeper, a gambler and a boxing referee, among his other mundane pursuits.[16]

Wild Bill Hickok was a gambler, a drunkard and killed a number of people during his life who probably didn't need to be killed.[17] Some of the outlaws of the period were truly nothing more than psychotic murderers.[18]

The use of force at that time and in that environment, by the lawmen of the day, was frequent and necessary, based on my readings on the subject. I recall one story, the source which now escapes me, of a posse finding their quarry (several wanted men) "holed-up" in a shack, unaware of the lawmen's presence. When one of the outlaws came out in the morning to fill a bucket with water he was, with no warning, shot and killed, in order, according to the member of the posse relating the event, "to get their (*the other outlaws*) attention."

The point of the above is; the lawmen of the period were basically untrained, learning their trade "on the job." The people they deputized certainly had no formal training in law enforcement (if such a thing even existed during this period in our history and out in the frontier), and, once "sworn–in," acted under color of law.

It was a model of law enforcement closer to the style imagined by our founding fathers than what was to evolve later.

The Latter Part of the 19th Century

As mentioned earlier, police departments formed in our nation were modeled after the English system. Initially the goal was multifaceted; the first aim was to maintain public order which evolved into the idea of having our law officers "fight crime."[19] One task that had to be accomplished was to develop some logical and useable manner people coming under the control of the criminal-justice system of the day could be identified and catalogued. The earliest widely used method was the Bertillon system (named after its inventor, Frenchman Alphonse Bertillon), whereby detailed anatomical measurements of the arrested were recorded and records maintained for future reference.[20] In practice the system was tedious to employ and not very accurate. Fingerprints soon replaced this method as a means of individual identification.[21]

I think it fair to state that the first effective attempt at developing a focused, scientifically based, investigative agency falls to the Federal Bureau of Investigation (FBI). This organization evolved into a professional, well thought out operation using carefully picked, educated agents who used the most up-to date investigative tools available. This included intelligence gathering, scientific investigation of crime scenes, and the interception of criminal telephone conversations. The head of the FBI, J. Edgar Hoover, proved to be a master in the art of generating publicity for the organization he started.

Local law officers quickly came to realize the benefits of becoming "fighters" in the war on criminality. Increases in budgets, enabling the securing of better equipment in order to accomplish this task, as well as having the public learning to depend on organized law enforcement for their protection, proved beneficial to law enforcement agencies.

It may be argued that our nation's law officers have strayed far from the original intent envisioned by our Founders. No longer were violations of law and public protection being handled by "citizens," but rather these tasks were evolving into a role handled by a specific segment of our society, the law enforcement officer. While, it may be that this has resulted in the loss of some of our freedoms, I cannot envision a smoothly functioning modern society without this specific task relegated to a relatively small group of specialized persons.

Further complicating any examination in regard the use of force and police authority, is the fact that there are so many different agencies at our state, county and municipal levels of government. In my personal experience the attitudes the police have toward the populations they serve varies wildly across the nation. For example, I served with the New York City Police Department from 1969 to 1990. During this period, among the tasks I was assigned, was conducting police training at the New York City Police Department's Firearms and Tactics Section. Contrary to popular myths surrounding police training, our goal, as it was explained to me by my commanding officer, Lieutenant Frank McGee, was to reduce both civilian and police casualties. From memory, when I started with the department, New York City police officers shot and killed approximately 330 (I recall this number from memory) persons a year in the city. Through training, and the use of sound tactics, this number is now measured, annually, in single digits (eight citizens were killed by New York City Police Department officers in 2013).[21] For a city the size of New York (8,400,000 inhabitants) that is a remarkable reduction in the loss of life.

I would like to offer one final thought in this chapter. I feel it important for citizens to understand that our nation's police forces hold no specific duty to protect individual citizens. The protection officers are required to give to society is just that, the officers are responsible to the greater society. Save for those situations where a "special relationship" has taken hold between officers and a citizen, officers have no special responsibility for the safety of individuals.

The following comes from my book, *Practical Handgun Training*:[22]

The police have no obligation to protect individuals

This is a difficult concept for most folks to accept, but it is fact. The United Stated Supreme Court has ruled that the police are under no constitutionally mandated duty to protect a person from harm. In that case a woman with a signed court-issued order of protection, lost her three children –they were murdered– to her estranged husband, yet the court found that the police were under no constitutional duty or obligation in the matter to protect her or her children (Castle Rock v. Gonzales).

There are some exceptions. One exists if there is a "special relationship" between the police and a person, or, if there is a state-created danger. None the less, there have been some disturbing incidents involving police (and fire department) failures to act, with no consequences to any of the responders involved. In one particularly grotesque case, both police and fire personnel simply watched a man commit suicide by drowning because the police and fire officers were in a budget dispute with their city. On Memorial Day, 2011, a suicidal man in San Francisco Bay stood in the water for an hour while onlookers begged the responding police and fire units to do something! When the man finally drowned it took a bystander to retrieve the body, as the fire personnel stated that their budget had not permitted them to have proper cold water rescue training!

Fortunately, most responding police (and fire) officers don't comport themselves as did the rather sad examples I mentioned above. None the less the reality is, for all practical purposes your immediate personal safety is in your hands.

*

The case law on police responsibility to ensure an individual citizen's safety is quite clear; there is none. One particularly unsettling case occurred in Washington D.C., the individuals involved (the victims of the crime) being three women; Carolyn Warren, Joan Taliaferro, and Miriam Douglas. The facts of the case are as follows:[23]

Two men burgled a residence occupied by three women. One woman, not yet discovered by the burglars, called the police (actually, during this crime the police were called twice!), informing the police dispatcher of the women's plight. She was told to remain quiet, the police would be there shortly. Although four police cars were dispatched the police never succeeded in locating the residence, leaving the area after one officer knocked on the front door and received no answer.

At knife point, Kent and Morse (the burglars) forced all three women to accompany them to Kent's apartment. For the next fourteen hours the captive women were raped, robbed, beaten, forced to commit sexual acts upon one another, and made to submit to the sexual demands of Kent and Morse.

The three women, who survived the ordeal, sued the Washington D.C. police department. In a 4-3 decision, the District of Columbia Court of Appeals affirmed the trial courts' dismissal of the complaints against the District of Columbia as well as those against individual members of the Metropolitan Police Department, based on the **public duty** doctrine. The Court explained that "[t]he duty to provide **public services is owed to the public at large**, and, absent a special relationship between the police and an individual, **_no specific_** *__legal duty exists__*." The Court adopted the trial court's determination that no special relationship existed between the police and appellants, and therefore no specific legal duty existed between the police and the appellants.

The court specifically stated; "The court states that official police personnel and the government employing them owe no duty to the victims of criminal acts and thus are not liable for a failure to provide adequate police protection."

The District of Columbia Court of Appeals, in part, wrote, "A publicly maintained police force constitutes a *basic governmental service provided to benefit the community at large* by promoting public peace, safety and good order." Furthermore, "The duty to provide public services *is owed to the public at large*, and, *absent a special relationship between the police and an individual,* no specific legal duty exists."[24]

Most United States citizens are unaware to the extent their personal wellbeing and safety is dependent upon their own resources. To a degree far greater than you might wish, you are truly, legally, and in a very real way, on your own in regard your personal safety.

References Chapter 1~
How Did We Get to Where We Are?

[1]*Are Cops Constitutional?*, Roger Roots, Seton Hall Constitutional L.J. 2001, p. 685
http://www.constitution.org/lrev/roots/cops.htm
(author's note; assigning specific page numbers to citations taken from this dissertation, save for the first page, is difficult, as the document was found on the internet, and does not show page numbers)

[2]*U.S. State and Local Law Enforcement Agencies Census 2008*: A BJS Report, Summer/Fall 2011, Vol. 28, No. 2–3
http://justice.uaa.alaska.edu/forum/28/2-3summerfall2011/f_lawenf_census.html

[3]*By the Numbers: How Many Cops Are There In the USA?*, by Daniel Bier, The Skeptical Libertarian:
http://blog.skepticallibertarian.com/2014/08/26/by-the-numbers-how-many-cops-are-there-in-the-usa/

[4]*Are Cops Constitutional?* Roger Roots

[5]ibid.

[6]*Colonial Trades*
https://sites.google.com/site/colonialjobs/night-watchman

[7]*The History of Policing in the United States, Part 1*, Dr. Gary Potter, Eastern Kentucky University, Police Studies Online:
http://plsonline.eku.edu/insidelook/history-policing-united-states-part-1

[8]ibid., part 2

[9]ibid., part 3

[10]ibid., part 4

[11]*Justice Story: How 'French Connection' heroin went missing from NYPD Property Clerk's Office,* New York Daily News:
http://www.nydailynews.com/news/crime/justice-story-french-

connection-heroin-missing-nypd-property-clerk-office-article-1.998525

[12] *Measuring Worth*:
https://www.measuringworth.com/uscompare/relativevalue.php

[13] *The Man Who Stole the French Connection*, Gangsters Inc.:
http://gangstersinc.ning.com/profiles/blogs/the-man-who-stole-the-french

[14] "39 The term "policing" originally meant promoting the public good or the community life rather than preserving security. See Rogan Kersh et al., "More a Distinction of Words than Things": The Evolution of Separated Powers in the American States, 4 ROGER WILLIAMS U. L. REV. 5, 21 (1998)."

[15] "47 *ALEXIS DE TOCQUEVILLE, DEMOCRACY IN AMERICA 96* (J.P. Mayer ed., Harper Perennial Books 1988) (1848)."

[16] *Wyatt Earp*:
https://en.wikipedia.org/wiki/Wyatt_Earp

[17] *Old West Legends, Wild Bill Hickok & the Deadman's Hand*:
http://www.legendsofamerica.com/we-billhickok.html

[18] *Badasses of the Old West, True Stories of Outlaws on the Edge*, Erin H. Turner, MJF Books, New York – (see various stories of outlaws of the period therein.)

[19] *Are Cops Constitutional?*, The War on Crime

[20] *Bertillon System of Criminal Identification*, National Law Enforcement Museum
http://www.nleomf.org/museum/news/newsletters/online-insider/november-2011/bertillon-system-criminal-identification.html

[21] *New York City Police Department Annual Firearms Discharge Report*, p. 15

[22] *Practical Handgun Training*, Richard Rosenthal, p.193

[23] *Remembering the case of Warren v. District of Columbia*;
http://www.mcfloogle.com/2014/04/16/remembering-the-case-of-warren-v-district-of-columbia/

[24] *Warren v. District of Columbia, 444 A.2d 1 (1981)*, District of Columbia Court of Appeals;
http://law.justia.com/cases/district-of-columbia/court-of-appeals/1981/79-6-3.html

Chapter 2~
Graham vs Connor ~ An Overview

For over a quarter of a century police officers (as a matter of law, probably anyone acting in an official capacity of governmental law enforcement authority, but this book, after all, is about the police use of force) have depended on the Supreme Court ruling which arose from the legal action, *Graham vs Connor*. This is the case where one goes to determine what right a police officer has to use whatever degree of force an officer uses in order to detain a person, arrest a person, use force against a citizen or, ultimately, to use lawful deadly physical force against another member of our society.

The consequences of this ruling has had a significant impact on every person living in the United States of America. In short, it gives our police officers the right to use force to the degree they, the officers, when viewing the activity before them, see as being necessary for them to use, based on their perspective as police officers acting in an <u>objectively reasonable manner</u>. It was a powerful ruling when decided by the Supreme Court and, I suspect, it may be one that the court will someday modify in light of what I have observed as our changing modern sensibilities in regard how our society wishes their enforcers of law to comport themselves.

I am not an attorney. My discussion of this important legal ruling will, therefore, be from the perspective of a retired police officer and laymen, as one who depended on the protections, and was guided by the limitations, this case offered to me, as well as, in a very practical sense how this rule also impacted the officers working under me while I served as a chief of police.

The facts of the *Graham vs Connor* case were never in dispute. Mr. Dethorne Graham, a thirty-nine-year-old African American man from Charlotte North Carolina, a man who had been employed by the North Carolina Department of Transportation, was a diabetic (he passed away in 2000).[1, 2]

On November 12, 1984, while at work in an auto shop, he felt the beginning of an insulin reaction coming on.[3] Mr. Graham asked a friend, Mr. William Berry, for assistance. Mr. Berry drove Mr. Graham to a convenience store to permit Mr. Graham to purchase orange juice in order to mitigate his diabetic reaction. The store was crowded and Mr. Graham could not wait to purchase the juice. He ran from the store. This raised the suspicion of a nearby police officer and the interaction between officers and Mr. Graham took place soon after. The police officers erroneously believed Mr. Graham to have been inebriated. The following quotes are from the transcript of Graham's testimony.[4]

"I said (speaking to officers), "My diabetic decal is in my pocket. All I have got to do is look at it." I was bending over trying to get my wallet out because my hands was cuffed. Somebody told me to shut up. I said, "Don't tell me to shut up because I'm trying to tell you what's wrong with me," and at that point somebody grabbed me from behind and slammed my head into the hood of Mr. Berry's car, and the next thing that I remember, I was face down, an officer on this arm, officer on this arm, officer on my left leg, and on my right leg, and they was carrying me to the police car, and one of them opened the door and threw me in like a bag of potatoes and closed the door."

"I asked that officer, "Please give me the orange juice." Her exact words: "I'm not giving you shit." And he (Graham's friend) went to the store and brought the orange juice back, and they refused to give me the orange juice."

"You have two broken bones in your left feet," and from there they told me to go down to Mecklenburg Orthopedic, and Mr. Berry took me down there and the doctor—" (there was further testimony regarding medical treatment for Mr. Graham)

After Graham passed out several officers then lifted Graham up from behind, carried him over to Berry's car, and placed him face down on its hood (Mr. Graham testified he was thrown into the back of the police cruiser "like a bag of potatoes." There was testimony that Mr. Graham had resisted being handcuffed. Regaining consciousness, Graham asked the officers to check in his wallet for a diabetic decal that he carried. In response, one of the officers told him to "shut up" and shoved his face down against the hood of the car. Four officers grabbed Graham and threw him head first into the police car. A friend of Graham's brought some orange juice to the car, but the officers refused to let him have it. Finally, Officer Connor received a report that Graham had done nothing wrong at the convenience store, and the officers drove him home, still handcuffed, and released him.

Under the "Graham" test, which requires an analysis of the totality of the situation officers find themselves in, several considerations were weighed. Among them:

➢ The severity of the crime at issue;
➢ Whether the suspect poses an immediate threat to the safety of law enforcement officers or others;
➢ Whether the suspect is actively resisting arrest or attempting to evade arrest by flight;
➢ Whether the force was "objectively reasonable." Whether the officer acted in good faith, or out of malice, is irrelevant.

Furthermore, this ruling makes it clear that the reasonableness of an officer's use of force is now, with this Supreme Court ruling, determined to be judged from the perspective of a reasonable officer on the scene, rather than through the clarity of well-informed hindsight.

We know now, of course, that there was no underlying crime involved in this case. None the less, it was reasonable for a prudent and responsible police officer to suspect some illicit activity was afoot when seeing a person quickly enter and then exit a retail store. It would be proper and correct for such an officer to inquire into the reason for this activity and the car stop conducted on the part of

Officer Connor (the officer named in the court ruling) certainly served that purpose.

Once contact was made with the person of interest, what ought to happen next would depend on a number of variables. Without prior knowledge of any illegal activity having taken place all an officer can do is question the person of interest and, if the officer has some reason to suspect a violation of law, detain that person until a determination is made, one way or the other, that some illicit activity had or had not occurred. Thus, Mr. Graham was detained, in handcuffs, pending the outcome of the officer's inquiry.

Clearly, Mr. Graham was acting strangely. Indeed, Mr. Graham was so agitated that his friend, Mr. Berry, asked Officer Connor to help Mr. Berry catch Mr. Graham, who was running around their auto at that point in the interaction. We know now Mr. Graham's actions were the result of a medical emergency.

During the interaction with the police Mr. Graham stepped away from his friend's auto and ran around the car twice, then sat on the curb and passed out. Unless an officer had additional information available to him at that time it would be reasonable for the officer to believe, certainly at least initially, that the person being observed was under the influence of some chemical substance.

The dilemma faced here is that once the officer (or officers) were informed of Mr. Graham's diabetic condition, and that there was identification on his person which would have demonstrated that he, in fact, had this medical issue, such a revelation should certainly have indicated to the officers his untoward actions could have also been the result of a diabetic reaction. However, in this case Mr. Graham was told to "shut up" and one of the officers stated they firmly believed this "mother fucker" was inebriated and not suffering from insulin shock.

As a laymen and a forty-plus year police veteran I ask myself, was it objectively reasonable for the officers to refuse to look at the medical identification in Mr. Graham's wallet which would have indicated he was a diabetic? The officers could have simply reached into the man's rear pant pocket, removed his wallet and examined whatever identification inside they wished. Even without knowing, for a fact, that Mr. Graham was a diabetic, would it not have been objectively reasonable for the officers to permit Mr. Graham to consume some orange juice? How would have such an act have compromised officer safety, save by them raising some highly inventive and imaginative hypotheticals?

Sergeant Brian Kowalski of the Tucson Police Department commented that by declining to examine Mr. Graham's wallet they forfeited a "Free look at his wallet." Stating Sergeant Kowalski's point another way, it is almost always useful for a police officer to avail themselves of all potential information available, as one never knows where such intelligence might lead.

In any case, *Graham vs Connor* is the current standard in regard how the actions of government law enforcement officials will be viewed when they use force in dealing with citizens and in officers compelling citizens compliance with the law.

The nine justices of the Supreme Court determined that the officers' actions in regard Mr. Graham were "objectively reasonable" when seen through the eyes of a police officer. Without taking into consideration the quality of the judgment exercised by these officers, this blanket protection removed any possibility for Mr. Graham, a person who had committed no violation of law, who had been physically damaged by officers (the court ruled that while Mr. Graham had a broken foot, this injury had not been demonstrated to have been caused by the officers), whose pleas for the most basic consideration on the part of the officers who had taken him into custody went ignored –indeed his entreaties to the officers, for them to simply take a moment in order to examine the contents of his wallet to demonstrate to the officers the veracity of his claims of his having a medical issue, only exacerbated the exorable behavior exhibited toward him by these officers– was left without recourse. Thus, as a layman, and without possessing the skills of an attorney, I must accept such actions as "reasonable."

Retired Chief of Police Anthony Bouza[5] believes the issue in regard the police use of force is not yet settled. He considers the ruling of *Graham v. Connor* to be a not well written, ineloquent and tortured attempt at justifying the actions of the officers involved in this incident. Summarizing his comments in regard this ruling, he stated:

"The great question it attempts to address is the police use of force. It is said that we are a nation of laws not men. That is a very significant statement. It means we come together, we elect leaders, we make rules, we insist these rules be followed or sanctions apply. And that applies to every human encounter of every kind. The use of force, by the police, so, under the fourth amendment, that no one shall be injured in their person or property except under due process of law applies. You shall be secure in your person and property and no warrants shall issue but for probable cause, a key phrase. The central feature of the law is objective reality. What is actually going on and what evidence is there to demonstrate what is going on? What conclusions can we make about what is going on as it relates to the law, to the rules that govern that behavior?"

During the give and take of the interview with Chief Bouza he shared some thoughts on the use of force by police generally. He stated, "A very important issue is, witnesses and citizens, observing the police use of force, really are unable to distinguish between the necessary and legal use of force and police brutality." None the less, the police use of force is guided by rules and by law. He used the example of weapons which would be considered unlawful for an officer to employ, mentioning "sap" (lead lined) gloves and switch blade knives (unlawful in some states).

I found it interesting that the Chief has no issue with the police use of the choke hold (and neither do I), a less than lethal method of subduing a recalcitrant person. When Chief of Minneapolis he had his officers trained in the proper technique for employing this hold.

According to Chief Bouza, police brutality begins when there is an end for the need to control a person and the need to use force to suppress violent behavior ends. When such behavior on the part of the person being subdued ends, the violence on the part of the police must end. Any violence on the part of the police beyond that point is gratuitous and constitutes brutality. He stated that the average person cannot tell you whether it is the 18th blow which is gratuitous, brutal and not allowed or whether it was the 17th or the 19th strike where the line was crossed. And the issue is, what degree of force is necessary in order to subdue and take control of a suspect, or someone mentally disturbed, who represents a danger to the public, the officers, and to themselves? Once that danger is abated and the person is under control the violence being used against that person by the police must stop.

Back to *Graham v. Connor*, Chief Bouza does not believe the supreme court had a "tight grasp" in regard the issue of the police use of force in this case. His reading of the ruling was that "Rules have to be enforced" but he found the court too bogged down, too tortured in their reasoning. Chief Bouza stated that the police conducted an investigatory stop but, as he read the material, did not conduct a meaningful investigation, a word, when used in this case, being an oxymoron in his opinion. In his view an investigation is an attempt to establish the circumstances surrounding a situation. In regard Mr. Graham, the officers jumped to a conclusion, they acted on that conclusion and they were completely wrong. And the

Supreme Court tortured itself to give the police the benefit of the doubt.

My review of the *Graham v. Connor* ruling, delivered by Chief Justice Rehnquist, showed that the mention of the words "sadistically," "sadism" and "sadistic" occurred thirteen times as did the words "maliciously," "malicious" or "malice." From my non-attorney point of view this makes me wonder what police actions were the supreme court attempting to justify in this ruling?

Richard Rosenthal

~References Chapter 2 ~ Graham vs. Connor~

[1] http://daughternumberthree.blogspot.com/2014/09/it-wasnt-reasonable-to-beat-dethorne.html

[2] *SOC320: Law, Society and Civil Rights*
ttps://soc320lscr.wordpress.com/2014/11/03/excessive-force-reasonableness-and-graham-v-connor/

[3] Transcript of Graham's testimony;
http://users.soc.umn.edu/~samaha/cases/graham_v_connor_tria_%20record.html

[4] ibid.

[5] Short bio of Chief Bouza found at the end of the book in:
Appendix of Persons Interviewed,

Chapter 3~
Mere Presence ~ Verbal/Physical Control

The old saying, "There's never a cop around when you need one!" is, I submit, erroneous. It would be more precise to state, "When a cop is around, you never need one!" Rarely, and most often only in the presence of a seriously emotionally disturbed person, would an individual act out in an inappropriate manner when in the presence of a law enforcement officer.

The mere presence of a uniformed law enforcement officer, when around the average citizen, brings on an assortment of emotions to those in the proximity to the officer. Indeed, when training new police recruits it is a routine admonition that when the officers are out in the field they should expect that all eyes will be on them. My analogy to my newest department members when chief of the Wellfleet Police Department was, the new officers exist in a fishbowl when among the public and they should learn to deal with this reality. The interest of those around the officer will vary from curiosity, through non-specific mild apprehension right up to a fear of being caught for some past misdeed on the part of a wanted criminal.

As a police administrator, I found that fully ninety percent of my problems arising from officer/citizen interactions did not stem from what the officers did, but rather, the issues resulted from what was said by them during the encounter. Not only did the officers words cause me angst, but in addition, to add to my conundrum, was the mingling of impossible for an administrator to evaluate facial expressions, tone of voice and officer body language included in the communication muddle, so as to make untangling the "he said, she said" give and take of such encounters and citizen complaints all but impossible to unravel by anyone tasked with evaluating the appropriateness of such interactions.

The words, "But chief, I just asked for her license and registration" relayed to me by my officer in a gentle, soothing tone of voice might well have been as professional and innocuous a request as suggested to me by the officer involved. Or it could have been an interaction containing a rude demand of "Give me your license!" combined with a sneer and a ripping of the license from the hand of the citizen handing the document over. Save for a video of the scene available for me to review (an option which I never had access to while chief of police), how in the world would it be possible for me to determine which of the three sides of the tale I could believe; the officers, the citizens or the actual facts?

That last bit of wisdom, of there being three versions to every story, is not as jaundiced a view of humanity as it might appear to be at first blush. It is common for people to see and hear things differently during the same encounter, for wholly honorable and non-malicious reasons. Sometimes this is due to expectations, such as that which a person might have after being pulled over when driving after committing a traffic infraction. Not infrequently racial differences come into play in regard how individuals hear what is said, as well as perceive subtleties in the tone of voice coming from the other party if they are of a different race. And sometimes the problem comes down to simple miscommunication.

I recall one incident when one of my officers pulled over a young African American woman for some traffic infraction. The officer, an even tempered, mild mannered individual, casually made a comment to her about her driving a nice car. She parlayed that wholly innocuous and non-malicious statement into a racially motivated questioning as to her ability to own a car of such high quality. Her ploy was successful and the moving violation was dismissed. My advice to officers after that incident was, be polite, be professional and don't engage citizens in unnecessary conversation when involved in an enforcement action. After a few such encounters it ought to be of little surprise that officers learn to comport themselves as automatons when interacting with citizens. You can't be criticized for something you said if you never said it!

Command Voice and the Verbal Challenge

Officers have, for many years, been trained to take charge of situations by using a "command voice." I believe this is a military term and soldiers are trained on how to best project their voices so that those under their control can be effectively directed. For police purposes the command voice is used to gain compliance of the subject without the need for the officer to use physical force.[1]

Verbal control has two components; first to identify the officer as a member of law enforcement and, secondly, to give instructions to the subject as to what the officer wishes that person to do. For many years, when challenging someone, it was most common for officers to yell out some variation of;

"Freeze!" or, "Freeze *expletive!*" or, "Police, drop the gun!" It was common for a series of expletives to be uttered by the officer as well, as if to highlight the significance of the officer's directive.

Although a person might think such orders are sufficiently clear for the average person to understand, police administrators found them lacking. While the admonition, "Freeze!" might be clear to some, what exactly does the word "freeze" imply the subject to do. Not moving would come to mind, but the New York City Police Department figured there might be a more professional way of informing the person of interest, who was being addressed by the officer, as to what specific action the officer wished that person to take. As for the order to "drop the gun!" that would, at first, seem like a good idea, unless the person in possession of the firearm is either a lawfully acting citizen facing an assailant, or robber, or an officer in soft (plain) clothes who is holding a criminal at bay. Dropping the challenged person's weapon might risk putting it in the

Richard Rosenthal

hands of the individual the responding officer ought to be most concerned with.

Around 1970 two members of the New York City Police Department Firearms and Tactics Section came up with a simple yet eloquent solution to the verbal challenge question, with their creating this unambiguous admonition;

"Police! Don't move!"

This command, especially when called out from cover, serves a number of purposes. It identifies the speaker as a police officer, it gives a clear instruction for the other person to follow, and, perhaps most importantly, it bought the challenging officer some time from a position of relative safety (from cover) so they could better evaluate the situation before them.

POLICE!!
DON'T MOVE

Misc. 1261

Rank-Name:_____

Shield No.:_____ Sqd. No.:_____

Those three simple words need further scrutiny and evaluation as they relate to both the potential use of force as well as the possibility for reducing the need to use force, while at the same time enhancing officer safety.

This Sticker is Found on Every Locker
within the NYPD

The reader might ask why is there the need to verbally identify the challenging person as an officer if that officer is wearing a uniform? There are a number of reasons this might be an issue. The first is, the ambient lighting may be so dim that another person might not readily see that the challenging individual is a uniformed officer. What about those situations where an officer comes upon two individuals involved in a confrontation and one of those people has

44

their back to the challenging officer? This is particularly critical should the person whose back is to the officer be holding on to a firearm or other weapon, as might be the case with an off-duty or plainclothes officer attempting to apprehend a criminal. Clearly, it would not be desirable for the person with the handgun to drop their firearm, permitting the "bad guy" to grab it. By stating to that person *"Police, Don't Move!"* gives the armed party time to identify themselves to the responding police officer.

The instruction we gave officers had an additional, very important element as part of this training. The instructors directed the officers, upon coming on a scene where there is a weapon involved, to issue this challenge from behind cover. Cover is defined as some object, material or thing which is resistant to being penetrated by gunfire. We told the officers that what we wished in regard this command was, besides offering the responding officers some significant protection from gunfire by them first taking cover prior to issuing the *"Police, Don't Move!"* command, was also to "buy them some time." Unless handed a script, which informed them of the facts of the event responding officers saw before them, the officers would have no idea who was doing what to whom when first arriving at a confrontation. Sound decisions cannot be made without responding officers gathering some information prior to acting. And the phrase "buy them some time" doesn't mean a protracted period of consideration and contemplation. Even a few seconds of evaluation will permit some initial communication between the parties involved and give the first responders a far better chance of determining the next appropriate action.

Dealing with the Mentally Ill and Emotionally Disturbed Population

A significant number of individuals' officers interact with, on an almost daily basis, suffer from, to a greater or lesser degree, some sort of emotional or mental health problem. How officers verbally interact with such people will have a direct impact on the officers need to use force in order to bring them under lawful control.

Regrettably, I have observed, from time to time, officers, while performing street duty, engage such disturbed individuals in a taunting or condescending manner. Almost invariably such an attitude exacerbates an already difficult and sometimes dangerous situation. My conjecture is, the officers do not wish to look "weak" or "soft" to their fellow officers.

Barking commands at a disoriented individual is unlikely to bring about the desired result of having them comply with an officer's directions. This is particularly true when the person being challenged suffers from some mental disorder, such as Alzheimer's disease. Yelling at them to do whatever it is the officer wishes them to do not only is unlikely to bring about the desired result (compliance) but might well cause the officer to use an inappropriate amount of force on that person due to the officer thinking that the non-compliance was willful on the part of the person being challenged.

It is believed that nearly 6% of the population of the United States suffers from some form of a severe mental illness.[2] Police administrators are tasked with ensuring that their journeymen level police officers have the proper training to meet the standards of the day. It would be impractical to train officers to a level of sophistication in regard the recognition of mental health disorders which a professional in the field would possess. None the less, some basic and fundamental concepts must be taught to officers so they might not only recognize individuals who have serious emotional (as well as medical) issues but learn to deal with such people in a productive manner, which does not automatically require the use of force to bring such individuals under lawful control.

It is common for officers to have them interact with people behaving "strangely" or "not normally" but who have committed no crime of any sort. Yet the officers may resort to the use of force, sometimes

Deadly Physical Force, to bring such persons into compliance with their directives. This puts the police in a legal quandary. How much force would it be reasonable to use against a person who has committed no criminal act?

Courts have looked at this issue and have come up with some suggestions:[3]

> What is the governmental interest in protecting the individual from harming himself?
> What is the individual's mental health?
> Did the officers know, or should have known, the individual had special characteristics making them more susceptible to harm from this use of force?

Furthermore, was this person posing a threat to themselves and was this person a threat to others?

George Thompson, of the Verbal Judo Institute, suggests people ought:[4]

> To be respected, not disrespected.
> To be asked, not told, what to do.
> To be told why.
> To be given options, not threats.
> To be given a second chance.

Having examined all the above it is important to keep in mind that should an officer come upon a situation which is exigent in nature, say a person, without warning, coming at them with a large and dangerous edged weapon, then, at that moment, all the Verbal Judo training in the world and skillful evaluation of the mental health state of their attacker would be of little utility. The action required would be immediate and likely result in serious physical injury or even death to the person brandishing the knife.

Sergeant Brian Kowalski, of the Tucson Police Department, has found that police administrators pay "lip service" to crisis intervention training. In his experience the dealing with emotionally disturbed individuals falls to line officers.

An example of one such interaction involving the Sergeant took place not that long ago. He and some of his officers were sent to a mental hospital. When they arrived, they found a person in crisis, who was suicidal. Yet, the call came from the very emergency room of the mental health facility where such an individual would have been taken. Fire fighters were already there, as was the medical staff, who were standing by until the police came. Sergeant Kowalski asked them why was this now a police issue, as where this patient was now situated, a mental hospital, was precisely where the Sergeant and his officers would have taken this psych patient to!

*

The variables which officers face in the field, as they relate to human interactions, is virtually infinite. Indeed, a citizen viewing an officer's use of force against a recalcitrant person would be seeing the "making of sausages." The actions are not pretty but the end result is desirable and necessary. For the police to be able to do their jobs requires that a good deal of flexibility be permitted officers' in their actions. So long as the officers' actions are objectively reasonable, such use of force would be within current legal standards.

References Chapter 3 ~ Verbal Commands

[1]*Verbal Commands*, <u>Police Magazine</u>:
http://www.policemag.com/blog/swat/story/2008/11/verbal-commands.aspx

[2]*Responding to Persons with Mental Illness*, <u>FBI Law Enforcement Bulletin</u>, Mason and Owen,:
https://leb.fbi.gov/2014/february/responding-to-persons-with-mental-illness-can-screening-checklists-aid-law-enforcement

[3]*Police Use of Force and Mentally Ill*, Policeone.com, Sailor, July 13, 2016:
https://www.policeone.com/investigations/articles/197080006-Police-use-of-force-CEWs-and-the-mentally-ill/

[4]*The art of Verbal Judo*, <u>Officer.com</u>, Miller, August 1, 2008:
http://www.officer.com/article/10248713/the-art-of-verbal-judo

Chapter 4~
Deadly Physical Force

"A Firearms and Tactics Unit's mission is to reduce both civilian and police casualties."

Lieutenant Frank McGee
Retired Commanding Officer
NYPD Firearms and Tactics Unit

There was a time when the average police officer carried a sidearm capable of firing no more than six rounds of ammunition. During my twenty years with the New York City Police Department, and for some time during my tenure as the chief of police of Wellfleet Massachusetts, I carried just such a sidearm. By the time I retired virtually every law enforcement officer in this nation was armed with a handgun which held between thirteen and eighteen rounds of service ammunition. This change in equipment –and potential degree of increased lethality– has had a profound impact on not only how the police use force, the degree of force which is used by them, but also on the public's perception of how that force is employed.

I do not wish for this chapter to be bogged down with too technical a discussion of weaponry. None the less, I would like to share two pieces of information with my readers; the first is, how has the technology of available firearms ultimately come to impact the police use of force and, second, what are the common misunderstandings the average person has in regard the ability of a handgun to stop –to immediately incapacitate– a determined attacker?

From the middle of the 19th Century up to around the end of the 20th Century law enforcement officers depended, for the most part, on six shot revolvers as their primary duty sidearm. This type of weapon, first seen in 1835 when Samuel Colt introduced a handgun remarkably similar in design to handguns still in use today, evolved over time. Although virtually all military entities adopted a different handgun mechanism when one became available at the beginning of the 20th Century, that being the semi-automatic pistol, military needs and goals were different from that of United States law officers.

The then new semi-automatic pistols (they "self-loaded" –after a pull on the trigger the handgun would be able to fire another round by simply pressing on the trigger, the weapon's action removing the spent cartridge and inserting a fresh one in to the firearm's chamber) discharged a specifically constructed type of projectile, generally one whose lead core was covered by a robust copper-nickel or other hard alloy cover. This was, and is known as, a full-metal jacket and, in the eyes of the military, this design solved two problems; the first was to ensure the reliable functioning of their troops handguns and, perhaps of more significance, such ammunition was in compliance with international agreements prohibiting the adopting militaries from the firing of projectiles which had lead exposed at the tips (because the expansion of the fired projectiles was not desired, for humane reasons).

By the 1980s various technological changes had taken place in the field of weaponry and ammunition. The first was the common introduction of handguns which routinely carried up to eighteen rounds of service ammunition within their grips (handles). Prior to this period only a very few handguns were capable of holding more than eight or nine rounds total. The second innovation was the development of pistol ammunition which could withstand the rigors of going through a semi-automatic pistol's action while at the same time being of a construction which permitted this same projectile to expand when impacting an adversary.

When I retired from the New York City Police Department my service handgun was a Smith and Wesson model 10, .38 Special caliber revolver, which held six rounds. I normally carried no less than twelve additional rounds on my person when working (or six additional rounds and another six-shot revolver). Shortly after I moved on to take command of the Wellfleet Police Department, the New York City Police Department adopted semi-automatic pistols which held as many as eighteen rounds of ammunition in the firearm. And that is the salient point; officers now carry sidearms which, without the need to reload, contained three times the amount of ammunition which had been held in the revolvers carried by officers only a few years earlier. A modern police officer may have, on their person, between the amount of ammunition in their sidearm and two spare magazines on their belt, upwards of fifty rounds of ammunition available for their use. This is a sea-change in the amount of available firepower the average police officer routinely possessed only a few years ago and has had a profound impact on how officers use force, the degree of force that is sometimes

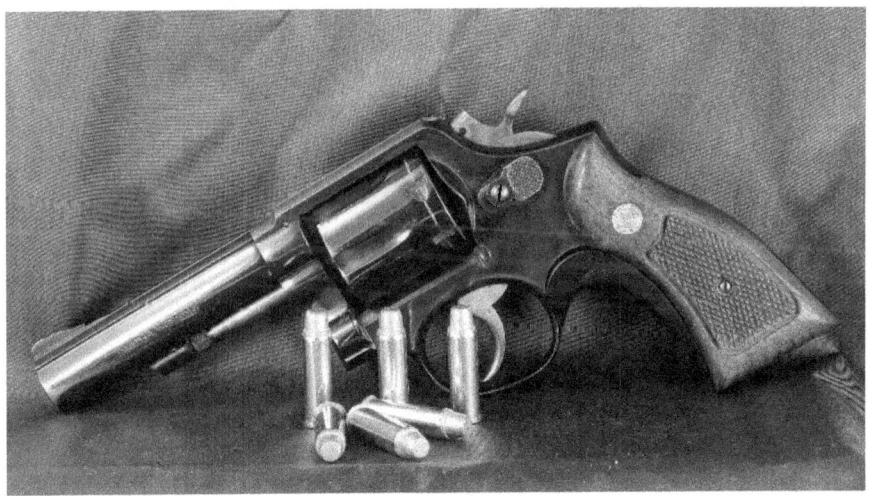

employed by them, as well as how the public perceives this use of force.

Smith and Wesson Model 10, Six Shot Revolver ~ Author's Service Handgun While in the New York City Police Department

When an officer fires his or her sidearm in the line of duty the average citizen has an expectation, based on what that citizen has witnessed thousands of time on television and in the movies; there is a near absolute certainty on the part of the citizen that whomever is struck by a handgun's projectile will fall back, be knocked off their feet and fly into the air. The person shot may crash through a plate glass window, and, if it is a vehicle being fired upon, the citizen will likely hold the expectation that the car will burst into flame, the vehicle's trunk will pop open, the auto's glass will be shattered and the car will come to an almost immediate stop. Alas, if we all had scripts to follow, life would be so much simpler.

Quoting from my book, Practical Handgun Training:[1]

"It is not practical, based solely upon a handgun's caliber and cartridge combination, to accurately foretell what the result would be when one person shoots another during a combat confrontation.

Handguns simply lack the power, and humans are too unpredictable in their ability to absorb physical trauma, for such to be a real-world possibility."

Glock 17 ~ 9mm Pistol ~ 18 Round Capacity

Please keep in mind that for every action, there is a reaction. Stated simply, if a firearm had the ability to physically knock a person off their feet, the resulting discharge would also cause the person firing that weapon to be knocked to the ground as well.

Permit me to state here that law enforcement has become embroiled in a *de-facto* arms race. When in the New York City Police Department I was taught that one of the measures used to determine the appropriate type of equipment to issue to officers was based on demonstrable data. For example, around 1970 the first "bullet proof" vests the department put out were designed to defeat three main calibers; the rather weak .22 long rifle, as well as the .38 Special and .45 ACP pistol cartridges. The reason those rounds were the ones the department was concerned about was because, when reviewing the calibers of handguns taken off the streets of the city by officers during this period, those were the most common handgun cartridges noted. Since then both the calibers carried by criminals and the kinds of the rounds found in them have evolved.

The Author at the 9th Homicide Zone; a S&W 6 Shot revolver on his hip, 6 Rounds of Ammo in the Pouch (arrow) and another Revolver, either worn on his Ankle or in a Cross-Draw Holster~ 18 Rounds Total

Times have changed. Once the revolver was the weapon of choice of criminals, now it's semi-automatic pistols. Thus, law violators now have the potential to have the same large number of rounds in their sidearms as do police officers.

Sergeant Kowalski commented that there has been a paradigm shift in how officers are trained in the use of their sidearms. He believes the increase in the number of rounds fired is less the equipment officers carry but more reflective of a change in training. His observation was, "Once it was shoot two and assess. Now it's shoot until "he goes away."

*

"Why do cops shoot to kill?"

I cannot imagine how many times I have I heard that lament over the years? The answer to the statement is a simple one; they don't shoot to kill. It would be a violation of law for a police officer to "shoot to kill." Police officers receive very specific training, which teaches them that their authority permits them to use that amount of force which is appropriate for a given situation, based on the objective reality of the threat as seen through their eyes as police officers. The degree of force an officer may use, depending on the level and degree of the threat that officer is facing, might rise to the use of Deadly Physical Force, which is that amount of force which is <u>likely</u> to cause death or serious physical injury. A police officer does not have the legal right to kill anyone. Only the state (the government) has that authority in our society, and that requires a person first be found guilty of a capital crime at trial and sentenced to death by the court.

The question as to when an officer (indeed, any citizen) may lawfully use Deadly Physical Force is a nuanced one. In simple terms the officer is required to be facing an adversary who must be able to meet three potential threats or criteria at the same time;

> ➤ Ability: Does the person the officer is dealing with have the ability to use that amount of force that is likely to cause death or serious physical injury?

> ➤ Proximity: Is this person close enough to the officer so that their ability to use this force against the officer is a viable, realistic threat?

> ➤ Manifest Intent: What are the actual intentions of the person the officer is concerned with, as demonstrated by the actions of that person?

Ability

The type of weapons capable of inflicting serious injury on another human are diverse. Common objects, not intended to be used as weapons, but fully capable of fulfilling that role, are found everywhere. Such objects such as a steak knife, hatchet, fireplace poker, hammer, baseball bat, pot of boiling water, an automobile, all those items, depending on how they are being employed, might well give a person the necessary tool, and thus the ability, to use Deadly Physical Force against another. In short, when an officer enters a person's home that individual is virtually surrounded by objects which, should that person so desire, have the potential to be used as formidable weapons against the officer.

The physical condition of the person making the threat must also be considered. A person whose mobility is limited to a wheelchair would be unlikely, save for unique circumstances (perhaps if they were armed with a firearm), to pose a threat to another person.

Proximity

The officer's adversary not only must have the ability to cause serious injury, but that person must be close enough so that such an assault is an actual physical possibility. For example, if an officer was standing on the sidewalk facing a person fifty feet away on the other side of a roadway, on the opposite sidewalk, and that person were simply holding onto a large bladed edged weapon but making no move in the direction of the officer, such a situation, while having the potential for a serious confrontation, would not yet have risen to the level of a Deadly Physical Force threat against the officer.

Manifest Intent

I used to teach this subject just using the word "intent." Some years ago I took a training class given by Massad Ayoob, a noted expert in the field of police training and the use of Deadly Physical Force. Mas pointed out that without considering the actual actions of the person posing the threat, seeing what they were actually resolved to do, it is not possible to know what that person's true intent was. Thus the term "manifest intent." What is this person actually, demonstrably doing that would indicate to another person (specifically, for the purposes of this book, as seen through the eyes of a reasonable police officer) that they pose a potentially lethal threat?

But here is the rub; when an officer comes upon a young person involved in some questionable activity, and that person pulls from their waistband a realistic looking "handgun" (indeed, an object indistinguishable from an actual firearm), yet an object which, in fact, poses no actual threat to the officer, does this demonstrate manifest intent on the part of the actor which would permit a reasonable officer to believe that the objective reality of the situation was such that the officer's life was in imminent danger? The answer to that conundrum, to me at least, is, yes, an officer would be justified in using Deadly Physical Force in such an instance. I am aware that would not lessen the public consternation such a shooting would generate.

"Why don't cops shoot for the arms or legs?"

When I was a youngster I watched that wonderful cowboy of the movies and television, Hopalong Cassidy, every Saturday morning. Hopalong, involved in innumerable gunfights, never ever killed anyone that I can recall. He always managed to shoot the gun out of the bad guy's hand, or "winged 'em" with a round to the shooting arm, putting the villain out of action. As an aside, I don't recall Hopalong ever permitting alcohol to touch his lips, nor his lips touch those of a fair maiden– either.

What I observed Hopalong able to do on TV was fiction, defying the laws of physics, human physiology, as well as sound tactical sense as it applies to the use of force and self-preservation. The reasons "shooting at the arms and legs" of a person posing a Deadly Physical Force threat against another person is impractical and unworkable is multifaceted:

> When humans are engaged in combat they are most often moving about. This almost always includes both parties involved in the situation. It would be, under such circumstances, quite literally impossible to successfully hit another person's extremities with a sidearm by the average police officer, especially when that officer was moving.

> If a person's arm or leg were impacted by a sidearm's projectile there is little physiological reason, save for unique circumstances, why such a wound would disable an opponent's ability to use Deadly Physical Force against the officer.

Police service handguns most often use projectiles which weigh approximately 115 grains to 230 grains. There are 437½ grains in an avoirdupois ounce. Therefore, a projectile might weigh from one quarter to one half an ounce. The human body (say a 180 lb. person) weighs 2,880 ounces or 1,260,000 grains. Even at the speeds which a handgun bullet normally travels, between 950 feet per second and approximately 1,400 feet per second (depending mostly on projectile weight) there is scant momentum transferred to the object struck that would cause that object to move, let alone be knocked down.

From a professional article in the *Journal of Legal Medicine*, "So the effect of the momentum transferred from the missile is virtually zero and there is no backwards motion of the person shot."[2]

Indeed, there are videos of people, while standing and wearing a bullet resistant vest (body armor) who have been struck by large caliber military rifle rounds and have shown virtually no rearward movement.[3]

In my book, Practical Handgun Training, I wrote:

"Having served in various functions within the NYPD, and, as stated earlier, the assignment most germane to this discussion having been that of homicide detective, I can accurately state that my empirical observations have been that once the gunfire starts there is no way to predetermine the outcome of the fight nor how the participants will react upon being struck by gunfire. I have seen the result of bullets bouncing off people (after striking various parts of the body, including skulls), I have observed people survive and fight on after multiple hits with heavy caliber handguns, I have observed the outcome of what would have had to have been defined as a "one-shot stop" of a young large healthy male, with a single .25 ACP round to the small of his back. In point of fact, an experienced police firearms instructor told me of a one-shot stop that resulted from a blank going off, the victim of this prank having fallen to the ground, crying out they had been hit!"[4]

The "hit ratio" police officers currently have in relation to the number of rounds fired, versus the number of hits on their intended targets, is around 15%. This number varies wildly, dependent on the department examined and which year is reviewed. The New York City Police Department no longer calculates such data (referred to as "hit percentages" by that agency) as that department believes the number is too unreliable for it to be of any value.[5] Said another way, for every 100 rounds discharged against persons by police officers, approximately 15 impact their intended target. Consider this, a gunfight is a fluid, emotionally charged, rapidly moving and evolving confrontation where some number of people are trying to strike other people with gunfire. Distances will fluctuate, the lighting conditions will vary from full daylight to the near absence of light and, from the moment the officer is aware there is a viable threat to their life to the end of the confrontation may last only a few seconds.

During those scant moments the officer is expected to identify the threat, determine the level of the threat, develop a tactical plan on how to deal with that threat and execute that plan. Should the officer survive the encounter the officer is expected to render first aid to anyone injured by gunfire (whether it is from his firearm or from someone else's), then give an immediate, accurate oral overview and report as to what transpired to a responding supervisor, then, soon after the incident, memorialize the action in a full and complete written report. I respectfully submit that is asking a great deal from a human being.

Sergeant Kowalski believes the actual trigger for the use of Deadly Physical Force on the part of an officer is their belief that, "Oh my God I'm gonna die!" The subtle nuances of the law are then shoehorned into their actions after the fact.

He pointed out that during such an exigent situation the officer is involved in an almost instantaneous decision making process and must decide what the next appropriate course of action should be taken at that moment. There's a lag time to the stopping of shooting as well. The last shot may well be unlawful, coming a fraction of a second after the justification for the use of Deadly Physical Force existed.

Sergeant Kowalski pointed out that with such extreme emotional distress as is seen during a combat confrontation, officers are subject to tunnel vision, auditory exclusion as well as the misperception of time. Yet our society expects and demands an almost super-human ability for a person involved in a life and death situation lasting a very few seconds to be coldly reflective of their surroundings and their actions. This is simply not realistic, as the input of information coming to the officer has been corrupted by their normal human reaction to such a threat to their lives.

At some time after the incident the officer will be interrogated in regard that officer's use of force. Should there have been the loss of life resulting from the officer's actions, if there is a video recording of the event each frame (literally) will be looked at, evaluated and critiqued by not only the internal investigators within the officer's agency, but by local prosecutors and, under certain circumstances, a Grand Jury. after which perhaps a court of law, civil, criminal (local as well as potentially Federal) or all three system of government, will again review the officer's acts.

Open Carrying of Firearms

Because the use of force so often comes into play when officers deal with an armed individual (or an individual who the officers believe is armed) I think this topic is worthy of discussion. Approximately forty-five states (see a breakdown of these states in this chapter's Reference section) have passed laws over the last twenty years or so which allow citizens to openly carry firearms when going about their normal daily business.[6] In many of these states such open displays of firearms includes the carrying of long arms as well. As might be expected, when citizens notice other citizens walking around their community with a rifle slung over their shoulder it is not uncommon for the police to be called and asked to investigate. Frequently the persons openly carrying these firearms have another person along with a video camera, their purpose it would seem would be to document the interaction taking place with the firearm carrier and responding law officers.

When this was being written I know of no untoward or criminal activity which has stemmed or resulted from the open carrying of firearms. Indeed, in Arizona where I spend my winters each year, I have noted a few folks going about their normal daily routines while armed with a handgun. Such sights cause me no concern and seem to be the accepted norm in that state. None the less, it may well be a cause of concern to a responding law enforcement officer having to deal with what may be a potential threat, yet which is an activity well within the law.

Speaking to Chief Anthony Bouza in regard this issue he stated, "Ours is a country of laws. If a person, wearing military camo type clothing is walking down the street, a fully loaded military style long arm slung over their shoulder (*an M-4 or AK-47 type of weapon*), so long as this person is otherwise in full compliance of legal statute, there is nothing for an officer to do. If that person declines to identify themselves, absent any other mitigating factor, then that too is not a cause for police action. The officer should simply leave. If the society wishes for people to comport themselves in such a fashion, it is not up to law enforcement to take any action under such a circumstance."

The Chief went on, "We must always look to the statute. If it's permitted, it's permitted. The officer must disengage. The officer faces the conflict of wishing for a desirable outcome versus facing the reality of life. If the law does not permit taking action, then the officer cannot act. If an officer does not have a legal basis to act, then the officer cannot take action. If the officer does not have the legal authority to compel compliance, then the officer must disengage."

Chief Bouza added, "Officers need not respond to the appearances of things – they need to respond to the legal reality of things. The law is in charge."[7]

The Ubiquity of Firearms

My good friend, retired Chief John Comparetto, has a saying; "Every time a police officer arrives at a call for service there is at least one firearm present. The officer's." Furthermore, access to firearms and the carrying of both open and concealed firearms, has never been so lawful or easy to accomplish by citizens in the United States. This presents a dilemma for officers. The non-criminal possession of firearms, during even routine police/citizen interactions, has officers very conscious of their likelihood of running into an armed citizen. Most of these interactions are benign. The citizen is exercising their lawful rights at the same time the officer performs their duties and all ends well. On rare occasions, regrettably, the contact between the armed citizen and the police officer results in a clash. Rarely do such events end well. For either party.

Technology to the Rescue?

One possible way to reduce the friction between police and the public is to find some way to bring people into compliance with lawful police directions and under legitimate police control while not having the officers needing to use Deadly Physical Force in the process. I think such an avenue might well be explored with the understanding that certain realities must be kept firmly in mind.

As I mentioned earlier, our nation is awash in firearms. At this time in our history it is not practical to eliminate an officer's ready access to a firearm for their own defense.

The only practical alternative would be a device which has yet to be invented. This "invention" ought to perform two functions; the causing of the near immediate cessation of threatening activity on the part of the officer's antagonist, as well as having the ability to perform such a function some reasonable distance from the officer.

Most lethal distances an officer "normally" faces during a lethal force confrontation begins at near contact proximity and on out to approximately twenty-feet from the officer (these distances are based on years of officer involved shooting data). An adversary armed with a handgun has the potential to cause death to an officer at ranges of over twenty-five yards (a trained, skilled marksman has this ability at much greater distances than that) and a person with a plain, commonly available "deer" rifle, say an old Winchester style 30'30 lever action long arm, has the capability of striking officers with a formidable, powerful round from over one hundred yards away.

While some such exotic anti-personnel or control device might well be within our near future technological capability for threats of a very close nature, situations which present themselves in excess of more than a few yards from an officer will still likely require the application of force by officers with the use of a firearm.

New York City Police Department Guidelines for the Use of Firearms

To ensure that officers use only the minimal amount of force, the Department has nine rules that guide a New York City police officer in his or her use of deadly physical force. They are as follows:

1) Police officers shall not use deadly physical force against another person unless they have probable cause to believe they must protect themselves or another person present from imminent death or serious physical injury.

2) Police officers shall not discharge their weapons when, in their professional judgment, doing so will unnecessarily endanger innocent persons.

3) Police officers shall not discharge their weapons in defense of property.

4) Police officers shall not discharge their weapons to subdue a fleeing felon who presents no threat of imminent death or serious physical injury to themselves or another person present.

5) Police officers shall not fire warning shots.

6) Police officers shall not discharge their firearms to summon assistance except in emergency situations when someone's personal

safety is endangered and unless no other reasonable means is available.

7) Police officers shall not discharge their firearms at or from a moving vehicle unless deadly physical force is being used against the police officer or another person present, by means other than a moving vehicle.

8) Police officers shall not discharge their firearms at a dog or other animal except to protect themselves or another person from physical injury and there is no other reasonable means to eliminate the threat.

9) Police officers shall not, under any circumstances, cock a firearm. Firearms must be fired double action at all times.

Let's examine each one of these admonitions in turn.

1) Police officers shall not use deadly physical force against another person unless they have probable cause to believe they must protect themselves or another person present from imminent death or serious physical injury.

This follows the current legal standard. Deadly Physical Force may, generally, only be employed in the face of a Deadly Physical Force threat.

2) Police officers shall not discharge their weapons when, in their professional judgment, doing so will unnecessarily endanger innocent persons.

While the underlying logic of this regulation cannot be refuted the primary purpose of such wording seems to me to be in place to permit an officer who decided not to use their sidearm to have a reason for not doing so.

3) Police officers shall not discharge their weapons in defense of property.

Once again, this section of the regulations recognizes current legal thinking. Property, of and by itself cannot be defended by the employment of Deadly Physical Force.

4) Police officers shall not discharge their weapons to subdue a fleeing felon who presents no threat of imminent death or serious physical injury to themselves or another person present.

A logical rule. Unless facing a Deadly Physical Force threat there would be little justification for an officer to resort to the use of such force. Exceptions do exist. For example, if an officer comes upon the scene of a shooting and the person who did the shooting flees, then the officers would be justified in using Deadly Physical Force to stop that person.

5) Police officers shall not fire warning shots.

This admonition has been around for some time. There are several reasons why the rule makes sense;

➢ "What goes up must come down." Discharging a firearm in a city always has the possibility for that stray projectile to do unintended mischief.
➢ When an officer fires their handgun, it is often not possible for other officers in the area to know who fired that round. Such a situation can lead to tragic officer misinterpretations as to the danger present at a scene.

6) Police officers shall not discharge their firearms to summon assistance except in emergency situations when someone's personal safety is endangered and unless no other reasonable means is available.

The logic of this rule is the same as for warning shots.

7) Police officers shall not discharge their firearms at or from a moving vehicle unless deadly physical force is being used

against the police officer or another person present, by means other than a moving vehicle.

Police handguns tend to be ineffective when used against a moving vehicle. It is unusual for a police handgun projectile to successfully penetrate the body of an automobile. Metal and curved glass surround the interior, all of which tends to deflect rounds unless the projectile strikes the surface at a close to 90 degree angle. Even should a police officer's round enter the cabin of an auto which is racing toward them, it has long ago been determined that a corpse at the wheel of a car makes for a terrible driver. The only rational, tactically sound thing to do when facing a vehicle headed in a person's direction is to step out of its way as quickly as possible.

I suggest there ought to be an addendum to this regulation. Should the vehicle be employed as a terrorist device used to cause mayhem, as has recently been the case in Europe, then officers must have the flexibility to fire into the cab of that vehicle in an attempt to stop the lethal rampage.

8) Police officers shall not discharge their firearms at a dog or other animal except to protect themselves or another person from physical injury and there is no other reasonable means to eliminate the threat.

Each situation involving a dog will be different. Most house pets, untrained in handler protection, are not a threat to people.

9) Police officers shall not, under any circumstances, cock a firearm. Firearms must be fired double action at all times.

There is a very legitimate reason for this last regulation. The New York City Police Department Firearms and Tactics Section studied inadvertent and unintentional firearms discharges by members of the department and, based on the data, determined that there were two main causes for such incidents:

➤ The cocked handgun, and,

> ➤ The officer's finger resting on the handgun's trigger.

Currently there are no handguns permitted police officers in the New York City Police Department which are capable of being fired "single-action" or while in a cocked condition. A handgun is in single-action, or cocked mode, when the hammer of the handgun (or striker if a pistol) is to the rear and the handgun may be fired with a relatively light pull of the trigger. A double-action pistol most often requires between ten to twelve pounds of pressure be put on the trigger prior to discharge, although some modern pistols have "safe-actions" which permit the pistol's discharge with pulls of around eight pounds. None the less, a safe-action pistol's trigger pull is substantially longer than that of a handgun using "single-action" mode of fire. A single-action handgun may need approximately three and a half pounds of pressure along with a very short trigger pull prior to discharge.

Police departments which issue handguns capable of discharge while in single-action mode are creating a terrible and unneeded liability for the department as well as for the officers assigned there.

References Chapter 4 ~ Deadly Physical Force

[1]*Practical Handgun Training*, 2014, Richard Rosenthal, p. 137

[2]*On the physics of momentum in ballistics: can the human body be displaced or knocked won by a small arms projectile?*, Int J Legal *Med*, September 1996, Karger and Kneubuehi:
https://www.purdue.edu/biomechanics/wp-content/uploads/2016/02/Karger_ballistics_Int_J_Legal_Med_1996.pdf

[3]*Video of man being shot with military rifle projectile in "bullet proof" vest*:
https://www.youtube.com/watch?v=dnnLgmNVQ5I

[4]*Practical Handgun Training*, Richard Rosenthal, p. 139

[5]*New York City Police Department Firearms Discharge Report 2014*, p. 55
http://www.nyc.gov/html/nypd/downloads/pdf/analysis_and_plannin g/nypd_annual_firearms_discharge_report_2014V2.pdf

[6]*Open Carry States as of 2016*:
Unlicensed open carry permitted	Thirty (30) States
License required for open carry	Fifteen (15) States
Open carry prohibited	Five (5) States

http://www.bing.com/images/search?q=Open-Carry+States+2016&view=detailv2&&id=D4F67EA77651AE69AD CA7493862D1D1DDD7ED4C1&selectedIndex=0&ccid=ahzsC1tf& simid=608040780416155652&thid=OIP.M6a1cec0b5b5f3d8a8c832 47f97a4dddao0&ajaxhist=0

[7]Interviews with Chief Anthony Bouza took place on September 7th and 14th, 2016

*

New York City Police Department Statistics

In 2014 eight (8) citizens were shot and killed by officers (8,400,000 population of New York City).

In 2014 there were 4,779 gun arrests in New York City.

Chapter 5~
The Rule Which Never Was

The Misinterpretation of the "21 Foot Rule"

Back in 1983 a police firearms instructor in the Salt Lake City police department, then sergeant Dennis Tueller (now a retired lieutenant from that department), promulgated a well thought out, elegantly simple and most useful training exercise, properly named the "Tueller Drill." Lieutenant Tueller, using a scenario he developed, demonstrated that a determined adversary, armed with an edged weapon, could, if running, close their distance to an officer facing them in a shorter period of time than could that officer unholster and discharge their sidearm.[1]

Tueller found that an officer, away from cover and with their sidearm secured in a modern police security holster, would require more time to unholster, aim and discharge their handgun than their adversary would take to close in on them with an exposed edged weapon.

Regrettably, and through no fault of lieutenant Tueller, his training demonstration became commonly and colloquially referred to as the "21 Foot Rule." By this quirk officers have, since the drill's inception, used the term "21 Foot Rule" to justify their use of force against individuals who possess virtually any type of knife, completely independent of Tueller's intent or even his structure of the scenario facing those taking part in his training exercise.[2]

Dennis Tueller set up the training exercise as shown below, with the following "givens" at the start of the drill (note, there are several variations possible when employing this exercise):

➢ The student officer stands exposed, that is, clear of any cover.
➢ The officer's handgun is secured in a standard police holster.

> ➤ Their "adversary" (generally another officer involved in the training exercise) stands approximately 21' from the first officer, holding a dummy (training) edged weapon.
> ➤ The "knife welding" officer charges the first officer and, generally, will be upon and "stabbing" the first officer before that officer can unholster and bring to bear their sidearm.

Even should an officer succeed in unholstering, firing and striking their adversary prior to the first thrust of their opponent's knife, the result would most likely be a "tie." It takes some time for a handgun projectile to have any impact (causing a cessation of activity) on a determined adversary, even when that round ultimately results in a mortal wound. Before their assailant might succumb to the gunshot wounds, the officer would likely suffer serious physical injury, possibly even death.

This exercise is truly a sobering reminder that action always beats reaction. Furthermore, a healthy determined adversary, holding an edged weapon, is a formidable opponent, armed with a weapon which never runs out of ammunition.

The mindset of quite a few people who go about armed is, as they are carrying a firearm they have nothing to fear. After all, sidearms, particularly modern police handguns with high capacity magazines filled with as effective anti-personnel ammunition as current technology allows, renders them impervious to harm and in complete control of their surrounding environment. This is, of course, nonsense.

In one case I was involved in, an officer justified his use of force (multiple ASP baton/metal rod strikes) against a confused, seventy-seven year old Alzheimer's victim, who at the time was passively holding on to a sheathed fishing filet knife with both hands, by referring to the "21 Foot Rule." In this particular incident, the officer:

➤ Upon arrival at the scene already had his sidearm drawn and pointed at the older individual.

➤ The officer started off from cover (his cruiser), then broke cover under his own volition.

➤ There had been no indication of hostile or aggressive intent on the part of the older person.

➤ The officer was the one who opted to close the distance to the older man, who was walking about in an aimless shuffle, while wearing slippers.

Retired Lieutenant Tueller first came upon the idea of this drill while conducting training with some new recruits. One of the officers asked the lieutenant just "how close is too close" when dealing with a person armed with an edged weapon, or a club, or some other type of "contact" weapon? Lieutenant Tueller wasn't sure but guessed three or four steps. He soon learned he had miscalculated the danger distance when he conducted a live experiment to see just how long it would take for one of his students to close the distance to an "adversary" in a second and a half, about the amount of time it takes to clear a police service pistol from a modern holster. That distance turned out to be around seven yards.[3]

The reason this time frame was used as the standard was because, through empirical observations, Lieutenant Tueller knew that was about the amount of time it took for an officer to draw, fire and hit a target at a distance of about twenty feet.

Lieutenant Tueller hoped this demonstration showed officers just how vulnerable they might be to a determined adversary who was permitted to close in on them while holding on to an implement that might cause them serious physical injury or death. Indeed, this exercise caused Tueller to reconsider the tactics of having officers just standing their ground, in the direct line of a potential attack.

Lieutenant Tueller never coined the term "21 foot rule." He spoke of danger zones and using cover, or obstacles, to facilitate slowing down an attacker. Other knowledgeable firearms instructors would, at various times, refer to his drill using other terms:

> The Tueller Principle/Tueller Drill; Massad Ayoob[4]
> Reactionary Gap; Caliber Press Street Survival book

But Lieutenant Tueller stated he thought that the "21 foot rule" was a poor use of terminology. He stated in an article he wrote on this very subject that words have meaning. He was concerned that a person might interpret a "rule" to mean that should a person with an edged weapon be fifteen feet away from the officer this would require or mandate the officer to shoot that individual. It followed that if the individual holding the edged weapon were twenty-four feet away from an officer the use of Deadly Physical Force would not be covered by the "rule."

Lieutenant Tueller was aware that there are many factors which must be taken into consideration before a police officer, indeed, any citizen, resorts to the use of Deadly Physical Force. Sometimes twenty-one feet is too close, sometimes the danger area is forty feet. What kind of weapon is the officer facing; a pen knife, a K-Bar, a machete? What is the manifest intent of the person holding the weapon? The decision to use force depends on the totality of the situation the threatened individual is dealing with at that moment.

To quote Lieutenant Tueller; ""Rule" has a nice catchy ring, but I think it is a very poor term. I would have never called it that. Your defensive tactics should be in response to whatever the circumstances dictate!"[5]

Lieutenant Tueller, at the time he developed this exercise, had been concerned with demonstrating the relationship between reaction and response. I use the phrase "action beats reaction" when discussing such things in my firearms training classes.

Lieutenant Tueller suggested that when an officer is facing a potential threat to consider moving to a safer position, preferably behind cover. If the danger is apparent, their sidearm should be out and ready. He has gone so far as to suggest that, if an officer can do so safely, taking several steps away from their attacker would be an acceptable technique when dealing with such situations.

So, regrettably, we have an excellent training exercise which has, through no fault of the person who first promulgated the training, evolved into an often misunderstood "recommendation" as to when, and when not, to use force on the part of officers.

References Chapter 5 ~ The Rule Which Never Was

[1]*Revisiting the "21-Foot Rule"*, *Police Magazine*, Ron Martinelli, Ph.D.:
http://www.policemag.com/channel/weapons/articles/2014/09/revisiting-the-21-foot-rule.aspx

[2]*The 21-Foot "Rule" Doesn't Exist, Calibrepress*, February 2016, Glennon:
http://calibrepress.com/2016/02/the-21-foot-rule-doesnt-exist/

[3]*The Tueller Drill Revisited, Armed Citizens Legal Defense Network,* Gila Hayes:
http://armedcitizensnetwork.org/the-tueller-drill-revisited

[4]Ibid.

[5]Ibid.

Richard Rosenthal

Chapter 6~
SWAT Units ~ A Conundrum

I think it important to understand a few things about Special
Weapons and Tactics (SWAT) units before jumping into the chapter.
First, and this is important, SWAT units, as a rule, do not initiate
raids prior to being called out for service. SWAT units are there for
line-officer support, are used by uniform and investigative police
personnel during particularly dangerous missions, tasks which
require highly specialized training and equipment on the part of the
first wave of officers or agents dealing with the situation. Prior to
SWAT utilization for a forced entry it is virtually axiomatic that a
signed warrant, affirming necessary facts first presented to an
impartial magistrate who, if satisfied, issued the warrant, based on
probable cause.

The reason this point is important to be aware of is because there
have been a significant number of SWAT raids, or police actions
attributed to SWAT units, where homes have been wrongly invaded,
innocent people –adults and children– have been injured, killed or
crippled, pets shot and trauma suffered by citizens who were on the
wrong end of such an incident. Almost by definition, a forced entry
entails the use of force both for gaining initial access into the
location but also for securing the people inside as well. A poorly
considered or improperly obtained warrant is simply the first step in
what could possibly spiral down to a tragic error.

Another matter which ought to be considered is the fact that there is
but a loose definition of what comprises a SWAT unit. The federal
government will state, truthfully, that only a single SWAT unit exists
within federal law enforcement, that unit being in the Federal Bureau
of Investigation (FBI). Yet, I clearly recall seeing video of the
Alcohol, Tobacco, Firearms and Explosives raid in Waco Texas in
February 1993 during that agency's attempt to enter the compound
of the Branch Davidians. A review of one of the many videos of the

event show the ATFE agents were equipped with all the gear associated with SWAT units; Kevlar helmets, military style outer garments, knee and elbow protectors and the agents were armed with an assortment of long arms and machine guns, among the weaponry they carried and used that day.[1] So, if my understanding of the federal nomenclature and definition of what a SWAT unit is, in fact, correct, this was not a SWAT raid. Whatever "it" was, it did not go as planned. Retired Special Agent William Buford was quoted as stating, "We were going to go in there, we were going to kick a little bootie, then we were going to ease out and be home before noon. It didn't work out that way," At any rate, more than a "little bootie" got kicked that day.[2] Eventually the FBI's Hostage Rescue Team (HRT) ended the siege, which resulted in an ultimate death toll of approximately seventy people, many of whom were children, who died inside the compound's structures.

My point is, if it has webbed feet, waddles, has feathers and quacks, it is likely a duck, regardless of the name arbitrarily given the creature. When law enforcement personnel equip themselves as would a "normal" SWAT unit member would, then there is little doubt much confusion can ensue.

Law enforcement agencies require access to specially trained and equipped personnel to best deal with unusual and difficult situations. These special groups are generally referred to as Special Weapons and Tactics Units, or SWAT units for short. In the New York City Police Department, such trained and equipped personnel are found within that agency's Emergency Services Unit (ESU).

It is important to keep in mind that our nation has, among any of the other first world countries, the most heavily armed civilian population. United States citizens, depending on the state in which they reside, may lawfully possess not only a cornucopia of handgun types, but also an array of long arms that go from .22 rimfire rifles used for informal target shooting and small game hunting up to .50

caliber Browning Machine Gun cartridge chambered rifles capable of accurately hitting a human-size target positioned more than a half mile distance from the shooter.

Please do not read more into the above paragraph than is intended. This discussion is solely concerned with how legitimate law enforcement agencies use force while being properly equipped to handle the anomalous situation of a deranged and otherwise dangerous individual, or some other person bent on engaging in criminal activity. Frequently such people will have available, and utilize, one or more of the myriad weapon types commonly available, whether obtained lawfully or, more likely, through illicit channels. Such individuals will not infrequently engage officers while at the same time they are securely barricaded against police intrusion.

Indeed, an unstable person, armed with nothing more exotic than a 30'30 caliber deer rifle, can hold responding officers at bay for a distance of several hundred yards from where that person has fortified himself. To take such an individual in to custody requires the services of a trained and properly equipped SWAT unit.

New York City has had the services of such specially trained and equipped members within that Department for many years, well before current day SWAT units came into existence. The specialized Emergency Services Unit (ESU) originated in 1930 and slowly evolved into the highly-trained cadre of officers who make up its personnel now.[3] SWAT, in the iteration as this type organization now commonly exists in other police departments, first came about in the 1960s, initially in Philadelphia, then soon thereafter a similar unit was created within the Los Angeles Police Department.[4] The number of such units has grown exponentially over the years.

Members of SWAT teams generally wear non-standard police gear, most often resembling combat outfits used by our nation's military. The reason for the visual similarity between municipal (and federal) special weapons units and military units is simply that the military mission can be, at times, of a nature which mirrors highly dangerous situations that require municipal police intervention. The equipment used by our armed forces can be useful and appropriate for specialized police use. This is equally true in regard some of the armored vehicles now being employed by our SWAT units. None the less, there is a line between how the United States military

handles problems and the mission municipal law enforcement is tasked with. Stated simple; "The military, to put it bluntly, is trained to vaporize, not Mirandize."[5]

A Modern NYPD Emergency Service "Truck"

The dilemma which has arisen of late over both the uniforms and vehicles used by these specialized units is this; have our nation's law enforcement agencies been too keen on not only emulating the equipment and tactics used by our military but sharing their appearance as well? Furthermore, the creation and use of such specialized units has grown dramatically over the last several decades. Indeed, there is even a magazine, *S.W.A.T. Magazine*, devoted to the subject, its advertisement stating the journal covers; weapons, tactics and training. Agencies as diverse as the United

States Department of Education and the Food and Drug Administration have such units.[6] The number of actual raids conducted by these disparate agencies are difficult to ascertain. I've seen raw data estimating there are between 40,000 and 80,000 such raids a year.[7, 8] I do not know if those numbers are accurate. To further muddy the waters, there are subunits of various agencies that equip their personnel with helmets, long arms and uniform styles

that make them appear to be, and have the function of, such specialized teams. These units frequently hold other titles, thus are not technically Special Weapon and Tactics units. Please keep in mind my earlier "if it quacks like a duck" analogy.

Another Vehicle Option in use by a SWAT Unit

I think it necessary to take a step back and ask ourselves the question; why SWAT at all? To me, having availed myself of the services of such trained personnel during my police career, and knowing several friends who have also depended on such properly equipped and trained officers, to assist them in the performance of their duties, the answer is obvious. When a law enforcement agency is called in to respond to a difficult, dangerous and unique situation, that unit's tactics, training and equipment might not be up to the task. Thus, the required specialized training, clothing, gear, weaponry and vehicles are all appropriate for use within special SWAT units. What I believe we ought to be asking ourselves is, can the appearance of these specially tasked civilian law enforcement officers be mitigated in some way to reduce criticism from the general public without degrading the protections afforded both citizens and officers by having such units available? Is a military style camouflage pattern SWAT uniform an acceptable image for a

municipal law enforcement agency to put out to the public? Should the common use of facial covering (the balaclava) be used as a matter of routine or ought the cloaking of an officer's face by such a wrap be reserved for use during those times it has some rational tactical value and relevance?

A SWAT Assigned Vehicle ~ Is this Practical and Appropriate?

It is my view that if some reasonable modifications are not made by existing SWAT units, then politicians, bending to public pressure, will make such changes for them.

For example, would it not be beneficial for our law enforcement agencies, for the sake of the agencies, to simply paint the outside of their armored vehicles in standard police colors, perhaps with the addition of the words "Rescue Vehicle" in large letters displayed on the side of the vehicles? After all, when all is said and done, that is the very reason these vehicles exist in the police equipment inventory. Would not such a modification defuse, at least to a certain extent, the concerns of citizens when they see such a vehicle on the street during their call-out and use?

Gear

Members of SWAT units are encumbered with a plethora of equipment when they turn-out. To the casual observer this gear might not be obvious. A partial list would include:

- Kevlar helmet
- Eye protection
- Face protection
- Bullet resistant vest
- Harness to carry various items
- First aid pack
- Prisoner restraints
- Radio and external mic
- Rope in bag
- Respirator
- Weapons
- Magazines for weapons
- Pepper spray
- Flashbang grenades
- Belt and holsters
- Ballistic shield
- Hydration system
- Assorted tools (Leatherman type and at least one knife)
- Flashlights/night sticks

➤ Video camera

I'm sure I've omitted some valuable pieces of equipment no SWAT member would want to go into action without. And I've made no mention of the various components which make up the officer's uniform and elbow and knee pads in that laundry list of "stuff." I don't know the weight of it all, but surmise it to be substantial.

Clothing

SWAT members will, by definition, be performing dangerous and vigorous activities which will require highly specialized protective uniforms. I would suggest these uniforms, to the degree possible, mirror the colors and pattern of their agency's standard patrol uniform. On the outermost garment the officers' names should be clearly visible.

There is no logical, strategic, or tactical reason why officers' names are not clearly visible on the outside of not only the clothing worn by SWAT members, but by police officers assigned to difficult and challenging assignments such as riot and crowd control. A simple patch of Velcro sewn into the outer shell of whatever is covering the officer's clothing (such as the harness holding their necessary gear) would permit a Velcro backed cloth name tag to be pressed into service easily and be of a construction which would be independent of the specific harness issued the officer.

Balaclava (Tactical Mask)

The stated reason the tactical mask is used during SWAT operations is to protect officers' faces from the effects of an exploding flash-bang grenade as well as to protect them against shards of broken glass when making a forced entry. In addition, their use during periods of extreme cold weather might well be necessary to protect officers' faces. None the less, once that part of an operation is over which might prove dangerous to an officer's face, or when on assignment during periods of nominal temperatures, the question

remains, why permit officers to continue to cover their faces unless such a covering is task related? This facial covering seems to have become a fashion statement. While I applaud the desire of officers in their desire to look smart while in uniform I am confident seeing their faces will not detract from their good looks.

Here SWAT members are seen wearing tactical face coverings of the type used to protect them against proximity to an exploding "flash-bang" grenade, shards of glass coming from a forced entry, or from extreme cold temperatures.

Armored Vehicles

Multiple NYPD ESU trucks patrol New York City daily. Inside these vehicles resides a cornucopia of emergency equipment as well as a plethora of weaponry and body armor. Each truck has, among the weapons secured inside, a compliment of long arms (rifles and shotguns), submachine guns, military style assault arms, gas guns and enough ammunition to hold off a small army. And that's a good thing. Plus, and this is my point, none of the over 8,000,000 residents and visitors in the city takes notice of these vehicles. That's because these ESU trucks are painted the same colors, and are adorned with the same markings, as "normal" NYPD vehicles. They are, for all intents and purposes, if not invisible to the average citizen then certainly indistinguishable from every other police vehicle patrolling the streets of the largest city in our nation, to the millions of people these vehicles pass by daily. Furthermore, ESU members come prepared to save your life as well as use force against you.

There is no rational, tactically supportable reason why an armored SWAT vehicle used by a municipal police agency need bring unnecessary attention to itself by being painted in a color more appropriate to that found adorning camouflaged vehicles seen in war

zones. There is no tactical upside to such paint schemes. Indeed, during any kind of police confrontation involving vehicles with this type of military style appearance, they soon become the focal point of media and crowd attention, which often works against the interests of the agency they belong to.

The Purpose of SWAT Members Covering their Faces when Simply Standing About Escapes me. Name Tags Would be Nice.

*

To reiterate, legal restrictions on the use of force by law officers are not waived when SWAT members are employed. Even during times of civil unrest officers must comply with the rules of conduct dictated by the law as well as by their department's policy. There are no logical reasons officers, even when specially equipped for unusual street or duty situations, should not comport themselves as do "normal" department members. If officers come to believe that the rules we live by are no longer constraining their actions, the results can be disastrous for not only the citizenry but for the officers as well.

I think it important to remember that one of the reasons this nation had a revolution a little over two hundred years in the past was in part because military personnel were acting as heavy handed law enforcement officers. I think it fair to state that several of our *Bill of Rights* amendments were a direct result of such actions. The British colonists that once made up our country fought a revolution to remedy that situation. Their concerns may be seen, at least in part, in various sections of our *Bill of Rights*:

Amendment II

A well-regulated militia, being necessary to the security of a free state, the right of the people to keep and bear arms, shall not be infringed.

Amendment III

No soldier shall, in time of peace be quartered in any house, without the consent of the owner, nor in time of war, but in a manner to be prescribed by law.

Amendment IV

The right of the people to be secure in their persons, houses, papers, and effects, against unreasonable searches and seizures, shall not be violated, and no Warrants shall issue, but upon probable cause, supported by Oath or affirmation, and particularly describing the place to be searched, and the persons or things to be seized.

Amendment V

No person shall be held to answer for a capital, or otherwise infamous crime, unless on a presentment or indictment of a grand jury, except in cases arising in the land or naval forces, or in the militia, when in actual service in time of war or public danger; nor shall any person be subject for the same offense to be twice put in jeopardy of life or limb; nor shall be compelled in any criminal case to be a witness against himself, nor be deprived of life, liberty, or property, without due process of law; nor shall private property be taken for public use, without just compensation.

Amendment VI

In all criminal prosecutions, the accused shall enjoy the right to a speedy and public trial, by an impartial jury of the state and district wherein the crime shall have been committed, which district shall have been previously ascertained by law, and to be informed of the nature and cause of the accusation; to be confronted with the witnesses against him; to have compulsory process for obtaining witnesses in his favor, and to have the assistance of counsel for his defense.

Amendment VIII

Excessive bail shall not be required, nor excessive fines imposed, nor cruel and unusual punishments inflicted.

*

Police officers, certainly many of those who are involved in SWAT units, bridle at the thought of anyone outside their specialty altering the equipment, the tactics they utilize or the authority to use the force they employ. I respectfully suggest they are mistaken. Reasonable people recognize the need for highly trained, specially equipped personnel to meet exigent situations which are beyond the ability, training and equipment provided of a journeyman level police officer to handle safely. The problem which has evolved is in the sheer numbers of SWAT units which have come into existence in law enforcement service (and of officers and agents who dress up in what appears to be such specialized garb) as well as the ubiquity of their deployment.

For such specialized units to continue to exist it will be necessary for some reasonable compromises to be made. If done intelligently these alterations will in no way diminish the utility of these units or inhibit them from performing their frequently dangerous missions. My fear is, if agencies dig in, refuse to modify how business is done, as well

as fail to understand that perception is an important part of a police agency's ability to function in our society, then people with no police background will prevail. Rules will be promulgated that will make the job of SWAT unit officers both more difficult and likely more dangerous. Some relatively minor changes as to how these highly-trained officers accomplish their missions would likely forestall such poorly considered changes to their protocols by people who possess neither the background, nor have an understanding, of the realities facing those assigned to such dangerous tasks.

This Photo was Taken after a Mexican Drug Raid. Such Weapons as seen here are Becoming More Common on United States streets.

References Chapter 6 ~ Special Weapons and Tactics

[1]*Waco raid videos*:
https://www.bing.com/videos/search?q=atf+waco+raid+video&qpvt
=atf+waco+raid+video&FO
RM=VDRE

[2]*Ex-ATF agents recall storm of gunfire ...,* Reuters, February 8,
2013:
http://www.reuters.com/article/us-usa-waco-atf-
idUSBRE9170JC20130208

[3]*Police N.Y.,* Emergency Services Division:
http://www.policeny.com/esdtrucks1.html

[4]*SWAT*:
https://en.wikipedia.org/wiki/SWAT

[5]*The Rise of the SWAT Team in American Policing*, NY Times,
September 7, 2014:
http://www.nytimes.com/2014/09/08/us/the-rise-of-the-swat-team-
in-american-policing.html?_r=0

[6]*The United States of SWAT?,* National Review, John Fund, April
18, 2014:
http://www.nationalreview.com/article/376053/

[7]*Are Police in America Now a Military, Occupying Force?*, The
Rutherford Institute, John W. Whitehead, August 05, 2013:
https://www.rutherford.org/publications_resources/john_whiteheads
_commentary/are_police_in_america_now_a_military_occupying_fo
rce

[8]"Eastern Kentucky University criminologist Peter Kraska has
published statistics suggesting that SWAT deployments in the
United States have increased from 3,000 in 1980 to nearly 45,000
during 2007."

Chapter 7~
Public Morals Enforcement

"Ought immorality as such be a crime?"

H.L.A. Hart[1]

"Public morals? The public has no morals."

Retired NYPD Sergeant John Mahoney

<u>What, Exactly, Do We Want Our Police Officers to Do?</u>

This chapter is less about the enforcement of public morals laws than in raising the question as to just what does our society wish our police to become embroiled in in regard the enforcement of such laws? There are quite literally hundreds of thousands of laws, statutes, and regulations on the books in our nation. Consider this; every law or regulation automatically carries with it the implied authority that the state can enforce these laws or regulations by force, with the possibility that such force could, under some narrow circumstances, escalate into a Deadly Physical Force confrontation.

I think it fair to say, and this is speculation on my part, that 99.9% of all citizen/enforcement interactions take place with no physical force being used by the government agency or representative to gain compliance on the part of the citizen in order to get that person to comply with the law or regulation in question. For example, a simple traffic enforcement interaction, between an officer and a citizen operating a motor vehicle, would normally have the officer approach the driver in question, ask that person for their mandated paperwork (most generally, with some variation depending on locale, their driver's license, vehicle registration and proof of insurance) and, once supplied with this information either permit the person to go on with their trip or first issue a summons for the particular infraction observed.

The potential for conflict arises when the vehicle's occupant, for whatever reason, chooses to challenge the officer and refuse to hand

93

over those documents, necessary to lawfully operate a vehicle on a public road, as required by the officer. Such a scene has become more common with a subset of the population who make claims to being "Sovereign Citizens" or "Moors" or some other newly created highly imaginative social entity. Somehow, in their view, a group not falling under the purview of this nation's legal system. Thus, instead of what ought to be a simple, brief, and rather perfunctory interaction with a law enforcement officer may turn into a hostile, and on rare occasions, deadly, conflict. Frequently the person making the (dubious) claims of not being required by law to have a driver's license, vehicle registration, proof of insurance or possessing any other valid authority to operate their vehicle on a public road will escalate the interaction by making a mind-numbing attempt at having the officer respond to a seemingly infinite number of pointless (often fanciful) questions as well as demands of the officer to recite the contents of arcane federal statutes in order for the officer to justify the officer's authority over the person stopped. The silliness generally devolves into demands for the officer's name and badge number, two pieces of information most often found on an officer's chest and, in any case, most certainly inscribed at the bottom of the citation being issued to the miscreant.

Thus, the fact that for every law or regulation put in place by government there is this potential for conflict ought to raise a question; are all the laws which have been promulgated over the past two centuries, most of which, once uttered, will continue to remain in force in perpetuity, truly necessary?

I wish to now voice a disclaimer; the enforcement of public morals laws is a beastly complex and nuanced subject. Every society on this planet holds forth with different values as well as shifting definitions as to what activities are socially acceptable and which are not only prohibited, but depending on the society involved, may well result in the death of those citizens found violating such expectations of the individual's social and moral comportment. For example, while pederasty may well be accepted in some societies (and not considered homosexual behavior, although taking place between an adult male and a male child), in the same society the crime of "adultery" might well be punishable by stoning the participants to death.[2] The range as to what is acceptable human behavior within the myriad cultural groups found on this planet is well beyond the scope of this book. Nor is it relevant to this discussion on the police use of force in our nation.

When does the maintenance of public order and the safety of citizens blend into the need to maintain public decency? When does the protection of the young meld into the prohibition of frowned upon activates by the prevailing segment of society and, indeed, what is the proper age for the "young" in question that they ought to be protected? The fundamental questions might well be; who does the activity annoy (and offend), who does it harm?

Brighter minds than mine have debated these matters for some time. No end to this discussion is in sight.

*

General Public Morals Enforcement

At the risk of drifting into areas of personal philosophy which I've developed after my forty-one years in law enforcement, I have come to wonder if the laws controlling what might best be viewed as the oversight of public morality, as well as of public decency concerns, are well thought out and useful for society to keep on the books as they now stand? The *Wolfensen Report* opined; "It is not the duty of the law to concern itself with immorality as such.[3]

Let us examine just a few such laws, some of which are currently found in our legal statutes, others which have either fallen into disuse or have been nullified or modified out of existence.[4]

For this purpose I interviewed retired New York City Police Department Sergeant, John Mahoney, who, during his tenure with the department, had worked both as a "white shield" plainclothes officer (a "white shield" officer is a patrolman – all men assigned to plainclothes during this period were of that rank) working out of the Manhattan South Borough office. Later he served as a sergeant in the 10th precinct dealing with public morals issues in a "conditions" car ("conditions" are any issues or problems, most generally at the precinct level, which tend to fall outside of normal police oversight and control). The period of John's experience in this area was from the late 1960s to the mid-1970s. His initial eloquent observation to me in regard the police enforcing public morals statutes was; "Public morals? The public has no morals."

The "normal" route for an officer first assigned to plainclothes was to work at the precinct level, then move on to division plainclothes, until, eventually, to be assigned to the Borough, which was an order of magnitude more lucrative (as in corruption and graft) than the units found below the Borough level.

John on the other hand started off in the Manhattan South Borough unit as he had a "rabbi" (New York City Police Department slang for a person with political influence and power. Also sometimes referred to as a "hook."). His rabbi was a man named Jimmy Reardon, a longtime plainclothesman, having served within the New York City Police Department from the 1940s through the mid-1950s. Reardon was also an author, a bookmaker and did some time in prison as well, a truly well rounded gentleman of the times. Reardon had sufficient power within the department while John was there to have John immediately assigned to the Manhattan South Borough. As an aside, John stated the only more lucrative position in public morals enforcement at the time was the "Bank Squad" (an assignment which had nothing to do with actual banking). Those were the detectives tasked with the taking down (enforcing the gambling laws) of "numbers" banks (the financial heart of bookmaking and gambling operations). John stated to me that the Bank Squad functioned as nothing more than shakedown artists.

John was clear in his view of the enforcement of public morals laws in New York City at that time. Such enforcement, as it existed, was in fact a "Boss's racket" (a boss being New York City Police Department parlance for a ranking member of the service). The sole purpose of enforcing such laws was to permit the police department's members to "shakedown" or extort money from those involved in these various illicit trades. He was adamant that, ultimately, it was those in the upper ranks of the police department who benefited the most from the money flowing in from gamblers and houses of prostitution. Every month the money was collected by "bag men" (those officers tasked with the job of picking up and handling the graft money from these illicit operations) which would be divided into "shares." A patrol officer might receive a single share, a sergeant two shares, a lieutenant three and on up the supervisory ladder. It was, indeed, "a Boss's racket."

John knew most of the bookmakers of the area since he had grown up in the same neighborhood he found himself assigned to as an officer, which, as a practical matter, reduced the need for extensive "on the job" training. His boss was Inspector Pierce Maher, who had been a drinking buddy of John's father. John described the now deceased inspector as having the "stickiest" fingers in the world. Maher instructed John not to make any arrests unless first checking with the inspector, a particular lieutenant (Maher's bagman – his collector of graft money) or a certain police officer from the unit. Again, the purpose of public morals law enforcement was not to eliminate those vices but to supervise, control and get rich off them.

When the Knapp Commission ended so did John's stint in Public Morals. Upon his being promoted to sergeant, John was assigned to the 10th precinct and within a short period of time the precinct's executive officer, then Captain Raymond Kelly (eventually to become Police Commissioner Kelly) made John the sergeant in charge of a "conditions" unit. Conditions were any problems that needed specific attention by the police, more often than not due to complaints by either politically connected or otherwise upstanding citizens. John, as luck would have it, had been Kelly's company sergeant while the two men had been in the Police Academy.

One of the first conditions that Kelly wanted John to deal with was the activities originating from several "leather" gay bars on the West Side of Manhattan, as well as problems arising from the actions of the local prostitutes in the same general area. At that time the 10th precinct boundary went north to a street just beyond Times Square.

Both John and Kelly were aware that the people on the street knew the cops "working charts" (work schedules) as well as, if not better than, the officers did. Thus, with Kelly's approval, John had the authority to work whatever hours he needed to get the job done.

A "kite" (a letter of complaint) had come in regarding two gay "leather" bars, the Spike and the Eagle. The patrons of those establishments dressed up to appear like stereotypical bikers, some even owned motorcycles. An organized crime guy, a tough "stone killer" who had already done twenty years in jail for a homicide, was the owner and operator of the most notorious of the joints. The issue at hand was this; Clients from his bar would leave the establishment and several dozen men would head to a place under the then raised section of the West Side Highway. At the time this was a major north/south roadway in Manhattan, and, once there, engage in, among other activities, a "daisy chain" – which is a group-sex activity where each male's sexual member would be affixed to another man's anus and, sometimes, to another man's mouth. The problem was, those driving past this bucolic scene, often families, were somewhat taken aback by the goings-on and wrote letters to the police department demanding that something be done to curtail this unsettling nocturnal pastime.

John was quick to point out to me that he had no issue with consensual sexual activates, of any sort, so long as they took place between adults and away from the public's view. None the less, once a complaint came to the New York City Police Department, and eventually worked its way through channels, some action at the precinct level would have to be taken. As mentioned earlier, such a missive was (and probably is to this day) referred to as a "kite."

So, as John knew the owner of the bar most directly involved in the aforementioned activities he paid the gentleman a visit. John politely asked the bar's manager for assistance in controlling the exuberant sexual pastimes of his establishment's patrons, to which the barman replied, if it ain't happening inside his bar, he didn't care what his patrons did outside, which was, to his way of thinking, now the New York City Police Department's, and John's, problem, not his. Somewhat stronger language might well have been exchanged during this mano-a-mano give-and-take of viewpoints.

John left and thanked the gentleman for his time, community policing having always been an important part of the mission of the New York City Police Department.

On a Friday night, soon after the fruitless discussion John had with the bar's manager, his team came in for an "eleven to seven" (11PM to 7AM) tour of duty. As John had anticipated, the actions causing public consternation were still taking place under the West Side Highway. John put his tactical plan into operation. He first went over to a local firehouse and requested the loan of some lengths of firehose. The firemen on duty were happy to oblige, inquiring as to what purpose this hose was to be employed? John responded, "You don't want to know."

Returning to the scene of the ongoing noisome public social interactions, John hooked up his hose to the nearest fire hydrant and proceeded to cool everyone down with a blast of pure cold New York City water. The power of the hose being what it was, John found that controlling the movement of the nozzle proved difficult and, remarkably, the stream of water struck and broke some of the windows of the bar with whose manager John had had the earlier unproductive conversation.

His attempt at enforcing public morals laws did not go unnoticed by the constituents of the offending bar as well as their allies. The next day, while John was at home, he received a telephone call from the 10th precinct, that there was to be a demonstration in front of the precinct that day, the purpose of which focused on one Sergeant John Mahoney, a "fascist" cop. The caller suggested that John and the rest of his team enter the precinct via a back entrance when coming in to work that day.

Sure enough, once back at the office John observed a substantial number of upset citizens in front of the 10th precinct who were carrying out a demonstration in his "honor." Curious as to what exactly was going on John had his team put on their uniforms (they had all been in soft clothes during their work dealing with the unwanted activities under the West Side Highway) and he and his team went outside to see what the fuss was about. However, before stepping into the fray John had the good sense to switch his name tag to someone named "Figueroa."

Once standing along the fringe of the demonstrators John asked one of the participants what the protest was about. He was informed by this individual about this "Nazi" cop named Mahoney and his predations upon the gay community of the area. John's suggestion to the demonstrator was to, "Keep it up, you might get rid of the guy."

John informed me that once he and his team returned to their office they thought it prudent to catch up on paperwork for the remainder of that tour of duty. As for the original condition that caused the local unrest, the problem never resurfaced.

Gambling

John's perspective was, and continues to be, that gamblers didn't bother anyone. Indeed, it was his experience that in a neighborhood with a bookmaker working there, there was less of a chance for criminal activity to take place in the area. Bookmakers did not want any problems around them. It was bad for business. And these were pretty tough guys, as were the people working for them. If there was an "issue" near them the problem person would be spoken to and informed that if they wanted to keep doing whatever was causing the concern, they should take their activities someplace else.

As with prostitution, gambling activity in the city was, during this period, effectively licensed by the New York City Police Department. Lest the reader believe the corruption stayed solely with the members of the police department, former plainclothesman James Reardon wrote that the money also went to judges, politicians and others within the criminal justice and social control systems of the city.

John pointed out that now that state governments have gotten into the gambling business with assorted lotteries (which he contends pay poorer odds to the players than do non-sanctioned bookies!), there is no longer any moral hi-ground for politicians to stand on in regard this matter.

Prostitution

Forty years ago, when I was a detective with the New York City Police Department, one evening I visited with John Mahoney at the squad room of the 10th precinct station house in Manhattan. John, still a sergeant assigned to the precinct conditions unit, was working the "pussy posse" (yes, that was in fact the colloquial term used by members of the department for the unit at the time). He was finishing his paperwork after having conducted a sweep of street prostitutes. There were two separate "cages" (prisoner holding pens) and in one I noted around ten or so assorted "hookers" possessing varies levels of pulchritude. In the other cage, alone, was a rather attractive young woman who I figured was also a common street walker. None the less, I was somewhat confused by "her" separation

Richard Rosenthal

from the other ladies until, after John noticed me eyeing this good looking chick, called out to me, "Rosie (my nickname), forget it. That's Charlie."

So much for my idle fantasies.

"Charlie" went by the name Diane. This person was not a street walker but worked as a high-end prostitute. Charlie (or Diane) was in the process of undergoing a full sex-change operation and John explained that Diane had no pimp. He first ran into Diane – remember, this was during the period when the New York City Police Department arrested people for selling pornography– when she worked at the Club Orgy, engaging in live sex performances involving two other women and a man (the other three being "junkies" who worked there in order to feed their heroin habits).

There are a number of arguments in favor of maintaining the illegality of the sex trade in our society. Street walkers (common prostitutes) tend to bring along with their activities assorted crimes such as larceny and robbery, not infrequently involving violence. Their pimps, in my experience, often have a rather choleric temperament. Thus, in consideration of those issues, and the fact that most "normal" folks don't really care to have semi-nude women (or males who appear to be women) hawking their "wares" on the streets of local neighborhoods, such prohibitions should, in my opinion, best be left in place.

What of the more sophisticated purveyors of sexual favors in the United States; the "call-girl" or escort service worker and the brothel worker (a trade which is legal in some parts of Nevada)?

There is little logic to attempt to eliminate the world's oldest "profession," a pointless as well as fruitless endeavor, when it would make far more sense to regulate, control and tax this business. The sensibilities of individual communities can be considered by their either permitting or forbidding such enterprises within their jurisdictions.

A licensed, supervised and taxed brothel would seem to me a logical way for society to manage an activity it's not quite comfortable with, yet which shows no signs of becoming extinct.

Controlled Substances

Morality laws and their violations frequently morph together. When working in Bronx Narcotics as a detective the team to which I was assigned went out one day to enforce our nation's drug laws. Our undercover purchased some illegal pills from an African American woman who, upon being challenged by another detective and myself, ran off with remarkable speed. Her flight was to no avail as we caught up to her and took our "prize" into custody.

At the station, it was required that a search be conducted of the arrestee. As this person was a female it was incumbent upon us to find a woman police officer to do the physical searching. Seeing our fruitless efforts to secure a female officer the prisoner volunteered that "she" was, in fact, a "he."

It fell upon me, as the arresting officer, to conduct the search. First the individual's top came off, exposing two well-formed and very feminine appearing breasts. The prisoner assured me all was OK and that the prisoner had undergone some medical procedure to secure said breasts. When I got down to this person's pants, when they started coming off all I saw was a triangle of pubic hair. I stopped the undressing process, once more questioning the sexual identity of the individual, who again assured me that I was, in fact, sitting "on the correct pew in the right church." He "untucked" his testicles and penis which were wrapped up in a sock and wedged between the cheeks of his buttocks.

Soon after I saw the notation written on the prisoner's "yellow sheet" (his arrest record) several collars (arrests) for prostitution in

Manhattan. Being of an inquiring mind I asked him about that part of his life. He explained that this entrepreneurial enterprise took place on the New York side of the Lincoln Tunnel, servicing mostly Caucasian commuters heading back home after a day's work. The majority of his clients desired oral sex. However, a small number of men wished for "straight" sex. The prisoner explained that in such cases he and the customer would go to the back seat of the now parked auto and, once the client was on top of him, the prisoner would arch his back and insert the customer's penis into our prisoner's anus, the client remaining unaware that the young lady he was having sex with was not, in fact, a young lady.

As a further aside, the prisoner mentioned that he lived with a heterosexual boyfriend. Which, to my way of thinking, simply demonstrates that life is a far more complex mix of humanity than we would all like to think it is.

Homosexuality

I mention homosexuality in the context of this book not because of current laws, but more as an examination of how such adult consensual actions had, in the past, resulted in law enforcement actions that, for the most part, served no rational public interest.

John Mahoney, when a sergeant in the New York City Police Department, was mandated, during one of his assignments, to enforce public moral statutes.

Public moral law enforcement stemmed, by and large, less from an objective evaluation as to how a non-sanctioned activity impacted the larger society but more from the sense on the part of the police hierarchy as to what the greater population felt was appropriate and proper public behavior. Said another way, the police were tasked with enforcing the public's perceived moral values. These, at best, are a moving target.

The dilemma we all face in such matters is, what activities are we as a people comfortable in taking place in public, and what activities should be proscribed for the protection of some members of our society?

By arguing that society has no legitimate reason to restrict any and all consensual adult activity leaves us with some potentially unpleasant possibilities. Should public fornication –male/female, male/male, female/female, or some other combination my lack of imagination leaves me unable to conjure up– be accepted as a "normal," if unsettling for some, open-air activity. Such goings-on are not as rare as one might think. There were, and certainly continue to be, "simulated" sexual activities during a few gay pride parades that I have seen videos of (these took place in Provincetown Massachusetts and New York City). As for heterosexual hijinks, I was told by a gentleman I am acquainted with that during a yacht "regatta" (whatever that might be) which he took part in he observed a number of ladies servicing various men while aboard quite a few of the vessels involved in the festivities, during mid-day and for all the world to see. Furthermore, in the same vein, the interactions of some celebrants which take place during Mardi Gras activities come to mind as being similar in nature.

Would it be best left to leave it to social scorn and public contempt in order to deal with public activities which otherwise make large numbers of the population uncomfortable? Would it be best to put regulations on the law books limiting such actions and therefore have such violations enforced by our police, as is now the custom? I see the potential for peril either way and, quite frankly, am uncertain in which manner society ought to best handle this rather delicate issue.

Richard Rosenthal

References Chapter 7 ~ Public Morals Enforcement

[1]*Devlin Was Right: Law and the Enforcement of Morality*, Gerald Dworkin, 40 Wm. & Mary L. Rev. (1999), p. 927:
http://scholarship.law.wm.edu/wmlr/vol40/iss3/11
http://scholarship.law.wm.edu/cgi/viewcontent.cgi?article=1563&context=wmlr

[2]*The Jerusalem Post,* August 1, 2016:
http://www.jpost.com/Middle-East/Taliban-stone-couple-for-adultery

[3]*Devlin Was Right: Law and the Enforcement of Morality*, p.929

[4]*I Walked Into a Nevada Brothel and My Expectations Were Shattered, Life, Business Insider*:
http://www.businessinsider.com/inside-a-nevada-brothel-2013-10

[5]*The Third Nation*, Rosenthal, 2015, p. 162:
https://www.amazon.com/Third-Nation-along-southern-border/dp/1514633752/ref=sr_1_9?s=books&ie=UTF8&qid=1480004670&sr=1-9&keywords=the+third+nation

[6]Ibid, pgs. 163, 164

Chapter 8~
The War on Drugs

"Well, here's another nice mess you've gotten me into."

Oliver Hardy to Stan Laurel

<u>Preface</u>

This chapter was taken, with some minor modifications, from my book, *The Third Nation*, a work about our southern border (mostly the area around Sasabe, Nogales and Lochial, now a ghost-town) and issues related to that part of our nation (and Mexico's). I point this out as there are references contained in it to both the aforementioned book as well as drug interdiction policies which I have noted in this part of southern Arizona.

The dilemma of our drug laws is that their enforcement results in a significant number of citizens being arrested and incarcerated for such violations, with no end in sight to ending this pernicious problem. Much of the enforcement of our drug laws involves the use of force, thus I think the inclusion of this material is most relevant to this book.

***

I don't like drugs. I don't care for people who abuse drugs. I am not pleased with the too wide use of drugs for entertainment or social purposes. Those are my personal opinions, based upon my having dealt with addicted personalities for so much of my law enforcement career. Chemicals used for recreational purposes rarely serve either their user, or the larger society, in a positive way. There are numerous types of drugs used for amusement and/or enjoyment by Americans today, ranging from the lawful –tobacco, coffee and alcohol– on through mild hallucinogens, to the opiates, synthetics and even the sniffing of glue and gasoline. There are so many substances used and abused by people in the United States that this chapter, and my comments herein, must be viewed in a very general way. After all, the purpose of this book is to examine the people who live and work along our southern border, it was not intended as a detailed overview of our drug laws. None the less, I have found it remarkable how much damage and danger human beings are willing to subject themselves to for them to attain some degree of physical pleasure, or how much money they are willing to pay in order to secure such a diversion. Even if it kills them. And drug trafficking most certainly does impact those living within The Third Nation.

I have a theory, which I am pleased to share with my reader. A century ago, had our nation prohibited the sale and importation of distilled alcohol but allowed the continued consumption of beer and wine, Prohibition would still be with us to this day. In my view that would have been a good thing, but we overreached and paid the price for our hubris.

I support the underlying premise of those who supported Prohibition; overconsumption of alcohol is bad for you and consuming distilled alcohol is very bad for you, for your family, as well as for our nation.

Permit me to refine my comments. Beer and wine are, arguably, foods. For thousands of years those liquids, along with boiled water flavored by tea leaves, were the only way to safely take in water, particularly in built-up areas, without risk of suffering serious physical illness. When consumed in moderation beer and wine enhance one's enjoyment of food and permits relaxation as well as more pleasant social interactions. I hold no issues with the moderate consumption of those two beverages.

Then there is distilled alcohol, a devastatingly dangerous, truly harmful, albeit widely socially acceptable drug.[1] I have seen many *old heroin "junkies" as a law officer, but a much smaller number of elderly drunks. Rotgut, a euphemism for cheap distilled alcohol, sees to that.*

When gin was first introduced into England several hundred years ago, the scourge it created in that society renders our concerns over illicit drug use today pale in comparison.[2]

The London gin cellar, Gin Royal, advertised with the slogan:[3]

𝕯runk for a penny
𝕯ead drunk for two pence

They meant it.

The dilemma our nation faces is, we've created a set of draconian laws, often promulgated for reasons of racial stereotyping, perceived issues of morality and bogus science, that has gotten us, and much of the world, into a terrible bind. The shorthand for this self-created conundrum is, the "War on Drugs."

Our anti-drug laws have evolved for over a century. They are, for the most part, not based on independent scientific observations as to the consequences of consuming any particular chemical, but more often the result of political expediency and bureaucratic venality.

Marijuana is the poster-child for such governmental abuse. Once again, my disclaimer; I do not "like" marijuana. No more than I "like" any of the recreational drugs. But I do not believe the deleterious effects of this substance warrants the time, effort and resources which our nation's law officers put into apprehending its sellers and users. Nor do I think it reasonable, or rational, to incarcerate people with long jail terms, for sale or use of this relatively innocuous plant product.

109

Driving about Arizona roadways, from time to time I'll come upon a Border Patrol checkpoint. Some have signs exclaiming, in large letters and numerals, the poundage of marijuana netted by that unit. The Border Patrol proudly takes credit for the tonnage of marijuana that agency's members seized, as if their actions were actually solving a problem. I'd like to offer up a modest proposal. With the next multi-tonnage tractor trailer load of marijuana that's confiscated by agents, the driver, under penalty of law, should be instructed to continue north, to the state of Colorado, where the sale of marijuana is lawful. Once there he would be directed to sell his load. The money would then be split in some predetermined, equitable fashion between the Border Patrol, to help pay for their services, and the growers of the marijuana. Rinse and repeat as necessary.

Keep in mind, what I'm suggesting is not particularly out of step with current United States government policy or philosophy. Consider, with the latest influx of youthful albeit illegal border crossers who, once "captured" by our Border Patrol, are eventually issued bus tickets, knowingly shipping them to homes of other people who are also in this nation in violation of our immigration laws, instructing the young illegals to present themselves, at a future date, for a hearing on their situation. According to news reports, fully seventy percent of those so directed have failed to appear for their hearings.[4] I was shocked, shocked, to learn of this.

Suffice it to say both our marijuana and immigration laws, and their enforcement, could easily be mistaken to be the products of Saturday Night Live script writers.

Drug abuse is a serious business, of that I am certain. I only wish we went about dealing with the issue in a rational, productive, non-destructive manner. To date, all we have done with our draconian and poorly thought out laws is to encourage the creation of the largest, best funded, and incredibly dangerous organized crime groups our world has ever seen.

We are repeating the history of Prohibition.

I suggest it makes more sense to put the weight of dealing with addicted personalities on the shoulders of medical professionals. Once a person is addicted to a narcotic (or any chemical for that matter) arresting and incarcerating them serves little purpose other than to ensure job security for law enforcement and corrections officers. Let the medical professionals deal with such people. This will save time, money and resources that could be put to better use.

You cannot legislate against habituation or long entrenched social customs and habits. This simply does not work and holds with it unintended consequences which create more problems than would be the case of simply getting addicted people on to maintenance level drug usages.

The use of illicit substances should not be viewed as a moral issue. You cannot pass a law that will have a practical impact on a person who is habituated to taking drugs. In point of fact, why ought we care if someone is addicted to some substance (ever try to wean a smoker off nicotine by cutting off their supply of cigarettes, or a dedicated coffee drinker from their several cups of daily brew?)?

Unbiased, objective scientific studies should be conducted to evaluate which currently controlled substances pose the greatest dangers to society (and their users) and deal with them based on those findings. Our current drug laws are largely founded on morality, custom and whether or not some substances, especially those which have been traditionally consumed by members of the dominant culture, are more socially acceptable than others. Alcohol is thought to be fine for general use, a chemical that is terribly

111

damaging to the human body, even fatal when taken in excess, yet a mild, relatively harmless hallucinogen such as marijuana is under strict sanctions, with the result that some people have been incarcerated for years for possession of this weed.

As is done with lawful recreational substances (alcohol and tobacco mostly) all such chemicals should be under government oversight. These materials should be controlled, regulated and taxed, as are the legally obtainable kinds.

Regrettably, the War on Drugs seems to continue to mainly serve the interests of three groups;

> ➤ *Major illicit drug dealers, with their positions of political power and wealth, are virtually guaranteed immunity from the consequences of meaningful enforcement of our anti-drug laws. Regulation, government control and taxation of illicit substances would reduce the value of their products substantially. Without the continuation of this nation's prohibition against drugs they stand to lose both wealth and power.*

> ➤ *Law enforcement is well served by our current laws. It certainly permitted me to have a long career. Enforcement agencies can appear to be "doing something" when interdicting low level drug mules or when arresting small time sellers and street users. Forfeiture laws permit law enforcement to secure windfalls of wealth with minimal effort, often with little or no evidence to back up their seizures. Corrections, due to the criminalization of what is arguably a medical problem, has become a major industry in this nation. Our rate of incarceration is unlike every other first-world nation on the planet.*

> ➤ *Our political leaders share in the benefits as well. They are able to pretend to be doing something positive in the "fight*

against crime" while at the same time promulgating laws which will ensure the problem will never go away.

We, as a nation, truly need to take a step back from this issue and come up with a rational solution to this dilemma for the benefit and wellbeing of all our citizens.

One very real concern our law enforcement leaders ought to have is the real potential for the coopting, by the bounty of money available to the drug criminals, those who are on the front line to protect us.

During my interviews with Nogales citizens I found a disturbing indication as to what might well be already taking place. This War on Drugs may have begun to influence some law officers in the area. I did not delve too deeply into the matter, the subject not being at the heart of my book. None the less, when citizens of Nogales Arizona informed me that, upon them witnessing the movement late one evening of large strange bundles being moved about by men in black outfits, these citizens called the Nogales Police Department. Twice. No officer ever showed up.

Corruption can take many forms. Simply not responding to an act of ongoing criminal activity is but one variation of this cancer.

References ~ War on Drugs

The Third Nation, Richard Rosenthal;
Available in *Amazon*:
https://www.amazon.com/Third-Nation-along-southern-border/dp/1514633752/ref=sr_1_1_twi_pap_2?s=books&ie=UTF8&qid=1482692674&sr=1-1&keywords=the+third+nation%2C+rosenthal

*

[1]*Distilled alcohol:*
http://en.wikipedia.org/wiki/Distilled_beverage

[2]*Gin:*
http://en.wikipedia.org/wiki/Gin_Craze

[3]*Beer Street and Gin Lane:*
http://en.wikipedia.org/wiki/Beer_Street_and_Gin_Lane

[4]Washington Post:
http://www.washingtonpost.com/world/national-security/us-most-new-immigrant-families-fail-to-report/2014/09/26/862520f0-4595-11e4-8042-aaff1640082e_story.html

*

News stories regarding massive quantities of marijuana interdictions:

http://www.arizonadailyindependent.com/2014/06/06/border-patrol-seizes-semi-truck-with-2-2-million-in-marijuana/

http://www.foxnews.com/us/2013/10/29/ton-marijuana-found-in-truck-after-traffic-stop-in-arizona/

http://www.borderlandbeat.com/2014/06/az-clone-government-truck-containing.html

Chapter 9~
The Officer's Dilemma

This is the chapter in which I've put together an amalgam of situations which officers either must deal with or are impacted by. Subjects I wish to discuss but are too limited for inclusion in the book in their own chapters. This is my way of saying the subjects contained here bounce around a bit, but, in any case, I wanted to offer them up to my readers for their consideration.

*

The Dilemma of Public Verbal Assaults on Officers – An Overview

The first amendment to the constitution, with few exceptions, permits virtually unrestrained verbalization of thoughts, feelings, emotions, political opinions and viewpoints on the part of citizens. I wish to make it clear that I have no quarrel with that protection, or indeed, any of the protections afforded citizens of our nation by that document. My desire is simply to address a situation which is making policing in our nation increasingly difficult, as well as to extend such protections afforded citizens by the *Bill of Rights* to our law enforcement officers.

I believe it fair to state that over the past decade or so there has been a general loss of respect for law enforcement in our nation. Fingers have been pointed to assorted "villains" some would like to hold responsible for this state of affairs, but I do not wish to engage in what would likely be a pointless debate. The reason I mention how the public at large views law officers has more to do with the nature of the interactions which frequently now take place between these parties. It is very difficult to conduct normal business in service to the public with someone who is acting out, spouting obscenities or is casting aspersions on an officer's race or ethnicity and, at the same time that person, or persons nearby, are memorializing the interaction with video camera or cell phone recording. This is the issue I would like to address.

For an officer working in the field, in order to gain compliance with the law (they are police officers, after all is said and done) the most logical progression for an officer/citizen interaction to take would be, in general:

➢ First have the officer show professional respect to the person they are interacting with, then,
➢ Diplomacy is then tried,
➢ After which the officer shifts to convincing the other party of the lawful authority the officer has over them.
➢ Should the first three elements fail to bring about compliance, then force may be used.

When in a courtroom, should someone there begin challenging the sitting judge, use inappropriate language (as determined by the judge), fail to take off their hat, or otherwise verbally defy the court, this person might well be held in contempt of court. Such a person could well face either a fine or jail time. I certainly see the logic and need to control the behavior of people coming before the bench. Not to do so would bring about chaos and disorder. I simply wish to point out the same may be said in regard police officers when they perform their legitimate duties.

I am fully aware that courts have found that the act of cursing at a police officer is protected free speech, as the person uttering the offending words is speaking to a government employee. It has always mystified me that when a police officer faces a verbally abusive individual this is deemed to be nothing more than their exercising their First Amendment right to freedom of expression. When such abuse takes place in front of a judge, it turns into contempt of court. I respectfully suggest this is nonsense. I have most often heard the admonition that "cops had to be thick skinned." Fair enough. Am I to understand judges are of a more sensitive persuasion? Indeed, a bit of reflection would seem to show that this is a rule created by the people in power, for their benefit. It is not logical. It is an unsupportable double-standard.

Before offering up my suggestions on how to deal with such matters I must toss in a few disclaimers. The first one being that my next series of suggestions flies in the face of how police departments have been managed for as long as I can remember. In addition, police administrators serve (with some exceptions) at the pleasure of civil authority. I think it fair to state that police administrators are not fully autonomous in their ability to deal with situations which will likely result in a significant public reaction.

None the less, times change and we must all evolve and change with society's demands, developing social mores, and expectations. I also fully expect my thoughts on this issue to be deliberately misconstrued, exaggerated and misstated by those who are opposed to my forthcoming suggestion.

None the less, I would like to offer a reasonable proposal which would permit officers a more nuanced way for them to interact with citizens. Police officers, indeed, all public servants, ought to begin their interactions with citizens in a polite and deferential manner. "Yes Sir, Yes Ma'am" are wholly appropriate –indeed, the preferred– manner in which to begin a conversation with a citizen. The issue I would like to raise is, what should be an officer's acceptable response to an unwarranted verbal tirade initiated by others and directed at them?

My proposal goes as follows. I have modestly named this model *Chief Rosenthal's Rules of Comportment*:

> ➤ Every initial interaction between an officer and citizen, save during some exigent situation, ought to be conducted from the officer's part in a professional, well-mannered and respectful tone. "Sir" and "Ma'am" being the preferred personal pronouns when addressing the citizen.

> ➤ Should the citizen decide that the nature and tone of the interaction would be a hostile, confrontational tirade filled with expletives, slurs and vulgarisms, the officer may, at their discretion, respond in whatever verbal manner the officer feels is appropriate for them to best control the situation.
> ➤ An officer may never respond in a way which involves the use of racial, ethnic or gender sensitive verbiage.
> ➤ Video recordings of police/citizen interactions, unless showing a violation of law on the part of the law enforcement officer, may not be used by the officer's agency for purposes of discipline.

After serving forty-one years "on the job" I'm already aware of the prevailing school of thought administrators have on this matter. The officer is expected to be a marionette, not to take anything said personally and to comport himself in a polite and professional manner even in the face of vile calumnies. This position is not particularly difficult to adopt when the person making such a decree sits behind a "bullet proof" desk (a "bullet proof" desk was a phrase I first heard from now retired Lieutenant Thomas McTernan, commanding officer of the New York City Police Department Firearms and Tactics Section. His phrase was to remind those of us making up the rules for officers to follow that, after all was said and done it was the line-officers who would be at the pointy end of the stick).

I disagree with the current standards restricting officer comportment for several reasons;

> ➤ A verbal assault is just that, an assault. It does no less, and I suggest perhaps more, damage to a person than a physical assault. The adage of "Sticks and stones may break my bones, but words will never hurt me." is both foolish and wrongheaded.

> A very strong response to a verbal assault has very likely stopped many a situation from escalating into a physical confrontation.

> When faced with an obnoxious, hurtful, epithet laced diatribe, officers frequently conjure up reasons to place individuals spouting such vile words under arrest, often with an end result of there being physical violence between the involved parties. Litigation frequently ensues with the taxpayers of the municipalities involved paying the bill.

Chief John Comparetto related a story which took place when he was a "street cop" in the Bronx, New York. The precinct he was in, the Four-Six, was a "busy house" (it was a high crime location with a wide diversity of ethnicities). The Chief and his partner, Gary –a skilled martial artist who taught the subject– encountered a large person involved in a domestic altercation. Chief Comparetto and his partner both initiated the contact as perfect gentleman; "Sir, please calm down." "Sir, please stop flailing your arms around." This composed attempt at defusing the situation only heightened the large man's belligerent behavior. Gary calmly said to Chief Comparetto, "It's time to introduce him to Uncle Louie." This was a code indicating the situation had now reached a potentially critical state and Chief Comparetto's ability with his coca-bola nightstick (his "Louisville slugger") was the next most appropriate tool needed in order to communicate with the large, angry, and out of control man.

Chief Comparetto knocked him out with a single blow.

As chance would have it an unmarked police car, containing two investigators from Internal Affairs, had been across the street during the entire incident. Once the body hit the ground the Internal Affairs officers pulled up and inquired of the two officers if the force used in this arrest had actually been necessary?

To Chief Comparetto's surprise the citizens around them sprang to his and his partner's defense, insisting the officers were not the

119

initial aggressors and who had spoken to the large man in a manner suggesting the officers wished to defuse the situation rather than exacerbate it.

If an officer were working in a quiet, low crime area then most certainly my newly conceived citizen/officer interaction technique would require modification. I'm thinking here of high crime areas with routine violence and general mayhem ruling the streets.

How might such an interaction between parties play out? First, an officer under my control would never be permitted to initiate the use of language that is unacceptable by today's standards (another moving target, but a real one nevertheless). Should the person they are attempting to communicate with respond in any one of an assortment of verbally abusive ways; challenging the officer's pedigree, race, intelligence, or simply resorting to the ever-popular expletive "Motherfucker," then I, as head of that agency, would have already instructed my officers they may then, in the spirit of enhancing dialogue with the community, respond in kind.

Many years ago, as a New York City detective I found myself embroiled in the mindless time-wasting exercise known as Manhattan "central booking" (the location where we completed our paperwork after an arrest and interfaced with the Manhattan District Attorney's office). While in line waiting for either photos, prints (fingerprint records) or yellow sheets (arrest records) –I no longer recall my purpose for being where I was at that moment– I noted a uniformed officer next to me wearing a most unusual sounding name tag, "MUFU." He saw my inquisitive look and volunteered this explanation; "MUFU must be my name, as that's what most people called me on the street."

There is theory and there is practice. Seldom do either agree.

Sergeant Kowalski suggests that, as a practical matter, rough and tumble police/citizen interactions already exist. He commented that while it would be nice to formalize some protections for officers involved in these types of interactions, "the politicians would never let it happen."

The Sergeant mentioned the use of the "tactical F-bomb" but stated that, "There are people who get the vapors when it happens," an amusing but accurate observation on the unreality of citizens' expectations when an officer is dealing with a potentially violent and difficult street person.

Sergeant Kowalski commented that our society has become accustomed to the Adam 12/Dragnet manner of police/citizen professional interaction, which has become ingrained and expected by most people.

Sergeant Kowalski reflected on the last Internal Affairs interview he was a party to. The complaint centered not on his "manhandling" nor sending a recalcitrant drunk to jail but rather was about the Sergeant's language, with the complaint being made by a non-involved citizen!

The more he thought about the incident the more irate he became, that this uninvolved person "took exception to the way I expressed myself" when taking police action. Which is my point; when an officer is embroiled in what can only be described as hand-to-hand combat their verbal interactions with their opponent should have no bearing on the matter, nor ought such language be weighed for the purpose of officer discipline.

I speak of this issue while being fully aware of some of the more sophisticated interpersonal communication techniques suggested to officers for them to better communicate with citizens. My personal favorite, and truly a most useful tool, is transactional analysis. Here officers are trained that when dealing with a person, to ensure that communication between the parties takes place, the interaction must be on the "adult" level (reasoned respectful discourse). Should one or the other party come at the other from either their "parent" (condescending, ordering, demanding) or from their inner "child" (tantrum throwing, yelling, unreasonable demands), then no communication would be possible.

There are times, however, where "reasoned respectful discourse" is not only impossible, but encourages more violent behavior. Each situation in this regard which an officer faces is thus unique.

People do not believe me when I explain that in my experience the most difficult policing, that part of enforcement which most likely brought about the worst behavior in citizens, were parking enforcement issues. When I worked as a homicide or robbery squad detective in New York City none of the individuals whom I placed under arrest for killing someone, or who had committed an armed robbery, ever accused me of harassing them or picking on them. On the other hand I have personally witnessed middle aged couples, due to them getting a parking ticket, throw a temper tantrum which would make a four-year old blush with embarrassment.

Traffic enforcement also tends to bring out the "evil" in many. There is a subset of the population who wish to "get back" at officers who have issued them a wholly appropriate moving citation. To that end officers have been accused of a wide array of improper actions. This includes the use of racial slurs, cursing, as well as accusations of improper touching of a member of the opposite sex.

Being aware of such problems my recommendation to officers was to minimize their verbal interactions with citizens during a routine traffic stop to a relatively brief "license and registration," along with a minimalist explanation as to the reason for the stop. And for them never to engage in a debate with the driver. The citizen can explain their concerns to the judge. This may fly in the face of the oft heard desire for "community policing" (a goal of policing sought after but one which is difficult to define) but I have found, over the years, that whatever the officer says will somehow be used by the other party in an attempt to make it sound as if the officer was acting improperly or otherwise doing some inappropriate thing.

Lastly, it is important to keep in mind what we are discussing here is custom and culture, not legal restrictions. Police administrators have created the constraints against officers voicing their thoughts when dealing with difficult people. There are no legal impediments to the use of such language on the part of an officer.

Therefore, I respectfully suggest, the rules regarding police/citizen verbal intercourse be changed, empowering officers to give as good as they are getting. To be blunt, failure to modify our police administrators current widely held admonition as to how officers may verbally control difficult street interactions will, eventually, leave those mostly high-crime areas of our nation virtually without police protection.

*

Car Stops

It's 2AM. A vehicle is doing 45 mph in a residential area which has a 35 mph speed limit and is pulled over by an officer. The vehicle contains two young males. The driver has a license and the vehicle is registered to his parents. There is no odor of alcohol emanating from the driver or other contraband material observed in plain sight by the officer. In that neighborhood, over the previous several weeks, there have been a number of house break-ins as well as several gang related drive-by shootings. The young man's residence is not in the area in which he was stopped.

The officer politely asks the driver where he was headed at this hour? The driver mumbles some words that are largely gibberish and which make no sense to the officer. This raises the level of suspicion the officer has in regard these two young men. He asks for identification from the second young man, who states, "I got nothing on me" and who refuses further comment.

At this point both young men tell the officer they wish to leave. What legal responsibility and what legal authority does the officer have in regard these two individuals?

The likely answer is, except for the option to issue a citation for speeding, very little. The officer may ask for permission to search the vehicle. If that is declined the officer might ask for a K9 trained in uncovering illicit drugs to come to the scene and not permit the vehicle to depart until the dog arrives and conducts a survey of the car.

I am unaware of any other lawful police related actions which an officer might take under such circumstances. Indeed, officers embroil themselves, and their departments, in needless litigation when overreaching their authority in an attempt to protect citizens from potentially dangerous situations.

As a point of interest, had such a scene played out a relatively few years ago, what would have happened is, the two young men would have been removed from their vehicle and "tossed" (searched). The inside of their auto would have been carefully gone over. All actions done in clear violation of our Fourth Amendment in the Bill of Rights (the prohibition against extra-legal searches of persons and property).

Today, an officer would have to be quite insane to perform such a perfunctory search. To do so would put the officer in serious legal jeopardy. Most current law officers are aware of the limitations placed on them by society and, as we are a nation of laws, these laws must be abided by.

*

Sovereign Citizens

I'm not sure when significant numbers of individuals in our nation decided they are not subject to most of our country's laws. Different factions who hold such a philosophy go by different names, the most common ones which I have seen are "Sovereign Citizens," "Natural Men," "Freemen," and "Moors."

As much of what is claimed by these folks is hard to understand and seems to be willful misinterpretation of our federal statutes, there appears to be a general pattern to their patter when interacting with law enforcement. Some of their thoughts and ideas may be seen below:

- ➢ The federal government has no authority over them.
- ➢ They are not United States citizens, although they enjoy all the rights of citizens.
- ➢ They are immune from paying taxes.
- ➢ They require no driver's license, vehicle registration or insurance.
- ➢ When stopped in an auto they will state they are "traveling" not "driving," which they will insist can only take place when engaged in commerce.
- ➢ Wages are not "income" because wages represent an equal exchange of labor (a form of "property") for money (another form of property), so there is no gain and no income(?).
- ➢ The tax laws cannot be enforced against citizens in federal courts, because federal courts are "admiralty" or "maritime" courts or (alternatively) tax enforcement is governed by admiralty law and can be defeated by properly invoking admiralty procedures.
- ➢ If the flag of the United States in a courtroom has a gold fringe, then the court is operating under martial law.
- ➢ A judge must be able to produce a copy of his "oath of office" on demand, and has no authority without it.
- ➢ A name that is written all in capital letters is different from a name written in mixed case (upper and lower case).
- ➢ Putting a comma or colon between your first and last names shows that you are a Freeman not subject to governmental authority.

> ➤ Using zip codes on the mail you send, or accepting mail with zip codes, is what subjects you to federal jurisdiction.
> ➤ The United States is not a government, but a corporation.

The above list of "beliefs" is but a fraction accepted as fact by members of such groups. Upon contact with a sovereign citizen, as might happen during a traffic stop, the officer will be bombarded with an innumerable series of bizarre statements and demands. If touched by an officer such individuals will scream "I'm being assaulted!" and or, "Rape!" as well as "I do not comply!" The verbal barrage will be non-ending. Such statements as noted below are the tip of the iceberg when interacting with such individuals:

> ➤ "As a man, what right do you have to stop another man?"
> ➤ "Speeding, in and of itself, is not illegal."
> ➤ "Do you have a warrant for my arrest?"
> ➤ "I'm not driving, I'm traveling."
> ➤ "I demand to see your supervisor!"
> ➤ Demands to see "identification." (which, when shown them, is never up to their standard)
> ➤ "Your firearm is upsetting me."
> ➤ "Am I being detained/Am I free to go?" (repeated incessantly)
> ➤ "The Constitution says ……" (whatever they are claiming is incorrect)
> ➤ You will be video recorded.

The verbiage is continuous, unrelenting, and never answers or responds to any of the lawfully asked questions put to such persons by law officers.

Should you attempt to physically take such a person into custody expect them to hold their arms out in a ridged fashion, effectively preventing you from placing their arms behind their backs without the use of significant force. While this is taking place, the arrestee will be shouting "I'm not resisting!" as they continue to resist arrest.

I respectfully suggest the proper manner with which to handle such individuals is as follows:

> NEVER ENGAGE OR DEBATE THEM IN THEIR REHTORIC!! If you do you will soon find yourself falling down the rabbit-hole of a non-existent fantasy world
> If a legitimate traffic stop is made for a clear infraction, ask them, three times, for their mandated documents required of them for travel on public roads (most often driver's license, vehicle registration and proof of insurance)
> Ignore their chatter!
> After the third request inform them that a refusal to comply will result in their arrest and the impound of their vehicle (again, dependent on jurisdiction and state statute)
> Failure to produce the required documents at that time should then result in arrest (as appropriate for the jurisdiction). **Get back-up first!**

When dealing with such individuals, use *EXTREME CAUTION!* They can be unpredictable and dangerous!

There are a number of videos available on *YouTube* which are able to give the reader a much better sense as to how these individuals comport themselves around law officers. I list a few in this chapter's reference section.

Demonstrations

Generally, by the time police officers are put in place as a barrier to the movement of demonstrators or for the protection of property, some incident generating public concern has taken place and feelings are running high with those citizens arrayed opposite the officers. As the police are the only people in authority which the demonstrators see or are in close proximity to, they become the target for the group's ire. If the media is present, the level of violence is likely to escalate.

Richard Rosenthal

The role officers play in these dramas is a difficult one. On one hand, people have an almost absolute right to voice their views. On the other hand, they do not have the right to violate the law. This admonition to stay within the law extends to assaulting police officers.

I have frequently seen news video of demonstrators coming face to face with officers assigned to demonstrations. Quite literally, their noses almost touching that of the officer standing before them. This is not acceptable. I'm unsure how this has come about but suggest that once a person comes within a certain distance to an officer (certainly within arm's reach) that person should be taken into custody.

During any major demonstration, the police administration should have arrest teams set up to deal with such situations. When a person comes into too close contact with an officer on the police line, as described above, the arrest team leader standing behind the officer should tap that officer on the shoulder. This would be a signal that the officer is to break from his partner, creating an opening for the arrest team. The arrest team should then, quickly, apprehend the person they are concerned with and pull that individual behind the line of police officers, taking them into custody. The line of officers would then close up once again.

I am less concerned about the eventual legal consequences of such an arrest than I am with preserving officer safety (and sanity).

Another issue occurring at demonstrations are the individuals there intent on antagonizing officers into using excessive force. Beside verbal taunts one common technique is for such individuals to carry "D" cell batteries in their pockets. From several feet into the depth of the crowd such provocateurs will throw their batteries at the officers. This almost always results in the officers venting their anger on the nearest demonstrators at hand, people who have not attempted to injure them.

Once again, police administrators must be prepared to handle such situations. Plainclothes arrest teams should be situated within the group of demonstrators, consistent with officer safety, in order to identify such individuals and arrange for their apprehension as soon as the situation permits.

How the Police Appear to the Public is Important!

I have mentioned this concern in my section on Special Weapons and Tactics Units. I hold that the less the police give the appearance of an occupying military force, the better the result for them. I'm not being "touchy-feely," I'm being pragmatic.

There is no logical reason officers, when serving during demonstrations, ought not to wear protective gear which is as close to the appearance as possible to "normal" police uniforms.

In short, this translates to:

> ➢ No camouflage pattern on uniforms, helmets, or related gear.
> ➢ The officers' names should be on the front of their outermost garment.
> ➢ No facial covering (balaclava) unless for a bona fide reason.
> ➢ No vehicles painted in military colors. All police vehicles within a department should be marked in similar fashion, and that includes specialized ones.
> ➢ Heavy weapons (long arms) should be best kept discreetly out of sight until such time as they are to be deployed.

As an example as to how we sometimes work against ourselves, there was a Black Lives Matter demonstration in Baton Rouge Louisiana where the photo of a tall, well dressed African American woman stood before a number of fully equipped officers wearing riot gear (see photo). I have no idea what preceded this confrontation, it is likely she placed herself in a position which required her to be taken into custody. Nor am I aware as to what transpired after she was

apprehended. None the less, this image did that police department no good.

Regrettably, once officers are arrayed in front of excited, upset, worked up and agitated people, the result rarely show scenes which put the officers in a good light. I suspect the best a department can do under such circumstances would simply be to try to mitigate against the most negative consequences of such interactions.

"Man with a Gun!"

The primary function of our police is for the general protection of the public. Indeed, court rulings have made it quite clear that officers have no specific obligation, or duty, to protect individuals, save for some "special relationship" existing between the parties.[1, 2] That is, should the police inform an individual citizen the police would protect that person from some specific harm, that would be an example of a "special relationship."

Here are some hypothetical situations, where most citizens would most probably believe that it would be reasonable for an officer, in fulfilling their responsibilities protecting the larger society, to compel an armed person to respond to reasonable directions from the officer. This for both the officer's as well as the public's safety. Would it not be sensible for a person so armed to be required to respond to reasonable questions put to them by officers, while the armed individual is being momentarily detained during a field interview. I don't believe such a legal authority, or protection for officers, currently exists.

The following hypothetical has actually taken place numerous times over the past few years. Police receive several 911 calls reporting either a man with a gun or people armed with firearms walking down a city street. Understand, in many municipalities the open carrying of firearms is not a violation of law.

Responding police officers arrive at the location and see several men; two carrying military style semi-automatic long arms and one

walking a few feet behind them videoing their route of travel.

Some Folks out for a Casual Stroll.

The officers politely ask the men their names and what they are doing carrying such weapons about on a city street? The men refuse to give the officers their names or show identification. One of the men pointedly asks an officer, "Am I being detained?"

What authority do the police have in securing these firearms and identifying the persons carrying these weapons?

I believe that the answer to that question is, under the circumstances I've outlined, none. These individuals are not in violation of the law and cannot be questioned without their consent or asked to surrender a lawfully possessed firearm.

The question I wish to raise is, in the above hypotheticals, shouldn't the police have the lawful authority to detain such individuals in order for the police to make reasonable inquiry into their behavior and to thus be better able to effectively protect the larger society? Furthermore, is it reasonable for people to be permitted to walk about with exposed military grade long arms in densely populated areas and then not be responsive to reasonable questions put to them by local police?

*

Officers do not start their day out planning on becoming embroiled in a physical confrontation. How such situations arise may be for an infinite number of reasons. I've attempted to outline some of the possibilities below:

> Under color of law, based on probable cause, the police are involved in a legitimate enforcement activity.
> Under color of law, based on probable cause, officers are involved in a legitimate enforcement activity. However, the person subject to the use of force had not committed the violation of law the officer believed they had, or any other infraction.

> ➢ Extralegal use of force by an officer without any basis in law. An unlawful use of force by the police.

Each of the above possibilities pose a potential problem for the officer using the force. Consider the shooting of an eighteen-year-old African American male in Ferguson Missouri as one example of a wholly legitimate use of force, in this case Deadly Physical Force, against a bona fide threat, yet which resulted in a major political upheaval not only for the police department and community in which it took place, but which also effectively ended the career of the officer involved.

An even more problematic situation can arise when an officer, believing they are legitimately involved in the enforcement of a violation of law, but after some investigation discovers they were in error. That is, there was no violation of law which would have otherwise legitimatized whatever force was employed by the officer.

Clearly the most serious issues arise when a law officer decides, for whatever reason, they desire to take some action involving the use of force, without there being any legal underpinnings for their conduct.

The Unlawful Use of Force

This type of situation creates the most problems for citizen, police department and officer. For example, it is very annoying for an officer, while involved in a legitimate arrest situation, to have an uninvolved party place themselves near to and in close proximity to the officer's activities, while at the same time recording the arrest. The dilemma the officer faces is, unless there is more to that person's actions than activating a video device (most often their cell phone) there is no violation of law taking place. The officer cannot do anything legal to remove this annoying person from the area. Regrettably, some officers ignore this fact and take such persons into custody, usually charging them with some variation of an obstruction of governmental administration charge (each state varies with the specific verbiage and title to such statutes) and, once force is thrown into the mix, usually add in "resisting arrest."

The majority of such cases are quickly disposed of when this person is taken before a magistrate, generally with an immediate finding of "not guilty" and they are released from custody. Shortly thereafter the videographer, or the arrested party involved, will likely, through an attorney, lodge a violation of civil rights lawsuit (*42 USC § 1983*) against the officer and department, which will probably prevail. Save for those instances when the use of force was so egregious as to have caused some serious physical injury to the plaintiff in such a case, generally a monetary reward will result. This money will not come out of the pocket of the officer who used poor judgment in their actions but rather from the taxpayers of the municipality involved. This is a less than perfect solution to the dilemma of how to administratively deal with officers who routinely use force without there being any rational or legal reason for them to do so.

One incident that I am aware of took place in a small Cape Cod town (I'm being deliberately vague). During a July 4th parade an officer who had a rather unpleasant and abrasive disposition decided that one of the parade floats band music was too loud. The officer attempted to have the musicians modify their sound levels. Regrettably, the officer did this in such a rude and obnoxious manner their actions caused a confrontation with the officer and the participants of the band. This resulted in a near riot in what was otherwise a bucolic and peaceful town! In other words, the personalities of those involved in officer/citizen contacts play a significant role in determining the ultimate outcome of such encounters.

Another incident took place when an individual, likely a person with a personality disorder, believed he was being followed by officers (I'm sure he wasn't). He went up to one of the officers (who was seated in his cruiser at that moment) and asked the officer why the officer was following him? The officer initially told the citizen he wasn't being followed and to get the heck away from him (more colorful language was used by the officer). This resulted in additional conversation between the parties until the officer had enough and, stepping from his cruiser, proceeded to beat the sawdust out of the annoying citizen and then arrest him for some silliness. All the while the citizen's cell phone was recording audio of the incident. The charges against the man were dismissed once he got to court. Here again, an officer with a strong personality permitted himself to be goaded into a wholly inappropriate physical confrontation, which resulted in a federal violation of civil rights complaint. As the officer retired prior to the case going to court it is the municipality which was left holding the proverbial "bag."

Erroneous Belief of Law Violation with the Use of Force Involved

It is very common for police officers to come upon a scene and, based on their initial observations, have a reasonable belief that the individual or individuals they are dealing with had committed some violation of law. Sometime later it then becomes evident that the officers were in error in their belief. Depending of the totality of the situation, most of these situations are explainable in a rational way so that once the situation is resolved there are no negative consequences.

When a homicide detective in the Bronx, New York City, I went out with a fellow investigator, Detective Bobby Stein, to sit by an apartment building in the hope that a man wanted by Bobby for murder would come out. It was a pleasant warm summer day. The location was within the Four-Six precinct and only a few days earlier there had been massive social disorder during a city-wide electrical blackout (July 13th~14th, 1977).

I was seated in the passenger side of the squad car and noted a young man, bopping down the street, a handcuff dangling from one wrist.

As he came alongside the squad car I quickly got out and took him into custody, cuffing his other wrist with the loose handcuff.

My thoughts were, this guy had somehow escaped from police custody. I put him in the squad car and we drove a few blocks over to the precinct.

The young man's story was, he had found these handcuffs during the turmoil of the blackout riot. That morning his younger brother had affixed one of the cuffs to his wrist, and the young man was headed to the Four-Six precinct to have the handcuff unlocked.

Suffice it to say, I didn't buy the story.

My partner, our prisoner and I made our way up to the Four-Six detective squad office and I began making telephone calls. First, I called "Central" (our main radio communications unit) and asked if there were any reports of a recently escaped prisoner in the Bronx. I was informed there had been none.

I tried a few more police venues, my goal being not to embarrass the officer who lost this prisoner. No luck.

On the handcuff's, I saw someone had engraved their initials in the metal. To make what would otherwise be a rather long story I managed to track down the rightful owner of the cuff's, fortunately working that day, who verified to me that he had, indeed, lost his pair of handcuff's during the blackout.

My "prisoner" had, in fact, committed no crime.

Once satisfied that I had erred, I went to the desk officer, a curmudgeonly lieutenant, and explained that I wanted to void the arrest I had just brought into the station. He was thrilled.

In short, I made out the appropriate paperwork, detailing the reason for my arresting the young man and the reason I was releasing him.

So, here was a pretty typical incident where a police officer had reason to believe there had been a violation of law. The officer acted on that belief, discovered his belief was in error, and rectified the situation.

No harm, no foul.

I might add, that was not the first time I had erred as a police officer, and it certainly would not be the last error I made as a lawman. Such is the reality of the job.

The real problem arises when there is a significant use of force against a wholly innocent party which results in either serious physical injury or death. One case in which such an event occurred took place during a SWAT raid on a suspected (likely actual) drug location. The officers, while gaining entry to the location, threw a "flash-bang" grenade into the room. The grenade landed in the crib of a one year old infant and the resulting explosion did horrific damage to the baby.

So, in this case, there is a legitimate police action which resulted in the use of Deadly Physical Force against a one year old child who committed no crime nor was in any way in violation of the law.

There was an incident in Indianapolis where a man called 911 during the early morning hours to report that his wife had been robbed at gunpoint. When the officers came to the man's residence the husband opened the garage door and was shot by one of the officers. The man had a lawful handgun in his possession, but, according to the news report had not raised the sidearm toward the officers prior to being shot. It is unclear whether a verbal warning was first given by the officer involved before the officer fired. Such a situation is a terribly difficult one to resolve. Officers arrive at the scene of an armed robbery. A man comes out of the home carrying a firearm. While I would have advised the officer to first take cover and challenge the individual, since I was not present I don't know if cover was available to the officer in this case. None the less, an innocent man was shot and there will be consequences.

Sometimes the use of force can be attributed to, for lack of a better term, bad luck. In New York City, a few years ago an armed robbery took place inside a small Bronx grocery store. Two of the victims ran from the store, right into responding New York City Police Department officers. One officer, either unintentionally or because of fear –the video is unclear as to what actually took place– fired a round killing the victim.

Probably the most difficult situations of all was of the kind that took place in Lebanon Tennessee. Police raided the wrong home, one next to the house which was the actual "drug house." The officers pounded on the innocent man's door. His wife, thinking it was a home invasion, yelled for her husband to get his gun. The sixty one year old man fired a shotgun round at the officers, who returned fire, killing the otherwise innocent victim of their mistake.

I've noted a pattern of reasons for such unfortunate encounters. One common statement from police administrators is that the innocent person "matched the description" of the actual criminals. Another is that the person injured had not followed the orders of the officer (as in reaching for something out of sight of the officer). Sometimes the reason for the use of force was the failure of officers to recognize a medical condition and mistakenly believe they were facing a recalcitrant individual when, in fact, the person before them had no ability to understand the officer's commands. And all too frequently insufficient intelligence is conducted prior to executing a warrant on a suspected drug house.

*

Police work is a complex mix of compassion, use of force and dealing with the ever-intractable, often difficult, ever changeable, rarely predictable human animal. The people officers encounter on a daily basis possess an infinite number of ideas as to how this nation's officers ought to conduct themselves, how much authority they should exercise and what laws, if any, they ought to enforce. As

President William Jefferson Clinton once stated; "It's never just one thing."

We, as a people, give our law officers a great deal of power over us. Sometimes that power is abused, but, fortunate, overall our police comport themselves in a reasonable, rational and humane way.

If we wish to remain protected by our police I suggest we must offer our law enforcement officers means to protect themselves from capricious, unearned vicious verbal assault and in some cases from physical attacks. Permitting our officers to be the "punching bags" of society is neither a healthy situation nor an acceptable way to treat those who we have tasked with overseeing the general well-being of our nation's citizens.

***

The Fantasy of Some ~ The Proper Role of Police in Society

References Chapter 9 ~ The Officer's Dilemma

[1] *Warren v. District of Columbia*, 444 A.2d. 1, D.C. Ct. of Ap. 1981

[2] *Castle Rock v. Gonzales*, 545 U.S. 748 (2005)

*

<u>Various YouTube Videos on the Sovereign Citizen Group:</u>

Sovereign Citizen Movement, Wikipedia:
https://en.wikipedia.org/wiki/Sovereign_citizen_movement

Sovereign Citizens Getting Owned – Compilation, YouTube:
https://www.youtube.com/watch?v=xUgmc7kKqOI

"Right to Travel" Debunked:
https://www.youtube.com/watch?v=uniJhnZYo6Y

Sovereign Citizen Training for Law Enforcement HD
https://www.youtube.com/watch?v=ALPs_n0WQaY

Debunking Patriot Myths Part 1 (four parts total):
https://www.youtube.com/watch?v=vTs_v8TAcoc

Appendix of Persons Interviewed

Listed Alphabetically

Retired Chief of Police Anthony Bouza:

Chief Bouza worked his way up the various levels of command within the NYPD, where he began his career in 1953, until retiring, in 1976, as a "two star" Chief, the Bronx Borough Commander, a veritable metropolis unto itself but politically one of the five boroughs of the city of New York having a population, at that time, of around one million souls.

From 1976 until 1979 the Chief was second in command of the New York City Transit Police Department, then a separate entity from the New York City Police Department (since merged). From 1980 until 1988 he served as chief of police for the city of Minneapolis Minnesota. Over the years, he has authored over a dozen books on assorted topics related to policing.

*

Retired Chief of Police John M. Comparetto:

Chief Comparetto, from 1973 until 2008, actively served in three law enforcement agencies, retiring as a Lieutenant in the New York City Police Department in 1999 (DEA Task Force), Director/Chief of the State of New Jersey, Division of Parole from 1999 to 2001 and Chief of Department Passaic County Sheriff's Department (New Jersey) from 2002 to 2008. The Chief continues to be actively involved in several police agencies as well as conducts training around the nation on Risk Management and Raid Planning. He holds the following degrees:

Master of Administrative Science, Fairleigh Dickinson University, 2005

Master of Public Administration, Marist College, 2002

Richard Rosenthal

Bachelor of Science in Criminal Justice, New York Institute of Technology, 1978

*

Tucson Police Sergeant Brian Kowalski

A member of the Tucson Police Department for twenty-two years, the Sergeant served nine years on patrol and twelve in his current supervisory role. He has performed as a Field Training Officer as well as a Field Training Sergeant, teaches at the Tucson Police Academy and is a Police Firearms Instructor.

*

Retired NYPD Sergeant John Mahoney:

Sergeant New York City Police Department, retired. Served in several units including undercover narcotics investigations and the Emergency Services Unit. Private contractor in Iraq involved in training and setting up Iraqi security forces.

Special Forces Group (rose to rank of First Sergeant in an infantry unit), as well as having served in the Marine Corp.

NY Institute of Technology, Westbury NY Bachelor's Degree in Criminal Justice

The retired Sergeant has attended numerous police and military training programs.

Author's Page

This photo was taken during a Wellfleet July 4th Parade. My wife, Frauke, served at the time on the Wellfleet Fire Department, for a total of seventeen years. I enjoyed telling people we had public safety all wrapped up in that town!

The author served for forty-one years in law enforcement. The first twenty was with the New York City Police Department, where he was assigned a number of commands. While at the rank of detective these included:

- ➢ Police Intelligence
- ➢ Narcotics Enforcement
- ➢ Homicide Squad
- ➢ Robbery Squad

When promoted to Sergeant and then Lieutenant, the author served in several others, including:

- ➢ Firearms and Tactics Unit
- ➢ Aviation Unit

While at Firearms and Tactics he was responsible for conducting the:

- ➢ Police Firearms Instructors School
- ➢ The Heavy Weapons Training Program, which encompassed:
  Heavy Weapons Training
  Detective Shotgun Training

Richard Rosenthal

> Cruiser Shotgun Training
> Undercover Firearms Training
> ➢ Research and Testing

The author also piloted department helicopters; Bell 206B and UH-1B models.

Author about to take the controls of an NYPD Bell JetRanger, 206B model helicopter.

After retiring from the city, the author took on the position of Chief of Police of Wellfleet MA, a beautiful town located on Cape Cod. There he served in a number of roles, including the town's Emergency Management Director as well as head of public safety communications.

One note about how this (indeed, all the author's books) are created. As the author is the result of a New York City public school education, his ability to construct grammatically correct prose is limited. Therefore, the author is completely dependent on his spouse who, raised and educated in Germany, acts as his in-house editor. She being far more competent in the nuances of English grammar than he is.